D0894652

KEYNES'S VISION

Keynes's Vision

A New Political Economy

Athol Fitzgibbons

CLARENDON PRESS · OXFORD

HOUSTON PUBLIC LIBRARY

HOUSTON PUBLIC LIBRARY

Oxford University Press, Walton Street, Oxford OX2 6DP
Oxford New York Toronto
Delhi Bombay Calcutta Madras Karachi
Petaling Jaya Singapore Hong Kong Tokyo
Nairobi Dar es Salaam Cape Town
Melbourne Auckland
and associated companies in
Berlin Ibadan

Oxford is a trade mark of Oxford University Press

Published in the United States
by Oxford University Press, New York

© Athol Fitzgibbons 1988

Hardback reprinted 1989
First issued as a paperback 1990

R0126140747
bstca

All rights reserved. No part of this publication may be reproduced,
stored in a retrieval system, or transmitted, in any form or by any means,
electronic, mechanical, photocopying, recording, or otherwise, without
the prior permission of Oxford University Press

This book is sold subject to the condition that it shall not, by way
of trade or otherwise, be lent, re-sold, hired out or otherwise circulated
without the publisher's prior consent in any form of binding or cover
other than that in which it is published and without a similar condition
including this condition being imposed on the subsequent purchaser

British Library Cataloguing in Publication Data
Fitzgibbons, Athol
Keynes's vision: a new political economy.
1. Economics. Theories of Keynes, John Maynard.
I. Title
330.15′5
ISBN 0–19–828641–4
ISBN 0–19–828320–2 (Pbk)

Library of Congress Cataloging in Publication Data
Fitzgibbons, Athol.
Keynes's vision: a new political economy /
Athol Fitzgibbons.
Bibliography: p.
Includes index.
1. Keynes, John Maynard, 1883–1946.
2. Keynesian economics. I. Title.
HB103.K47F58 1988   330.15′6—dc19   88–1887
ISBN 0–19–828641–4
ISBN 0–19–828320–4 (Pbk)

Printed and bound in
Great Britain by Biddles Ltd,
Guildford and King's Lynn

Preface

By Keynes's 'vision', I refer to what can be drawn from his *Collected Writings* and early writings, the vision of the public man. Many writers say that Keynes often did not mean what he said; others argue that he did indeed mean what he said, and that the depth of his ideas has simply not been recognized. I sympathize with the latter school, but I do not enter into the issue. I simply take what has been said on its own merits, on the ground that it is in the public domain. For this reason, and because my interpretation of Keynes is often at odds with the orthodoxy, I have stuck closely to the texts at points, though Keynes's early philosophy was often cast in formularistic terms, and the ideas in it might have been conveyed in a more simple and direct manner.

Initially, I meant to show that there is an idealistic strain in Keynes that has been unrecognized, but has had a large influence upon his economics. As this book progressed, it became possible to be more definitive; Keynes's economics and politics revolve around a specific ideal to which they are attached by a particular logical method.

In the previous five years there has been some important and fundamental scholarship concerning the meaning of Keynes, including Robert Skidelsky's analysis of his early philosophy and various studies, often associated with Cambridge University, concerning Keynes's theory of probability. I show that these and other interpretations of Keynes fall into a pattern if they are reinterpreted to allow for his idealism. When this is done, a well defined picture emerges which accounts for many otherwise puzzling aspects of both his economics and his politics. This is Keynes's philosophy of practical action, a well defined and logical organ of thought, unrecognized, new to the world so far as I know and ranging from a metaphysical idea down to immediate rules of decision.

When this picture first became apparent, I decided to lay aside my own less interesting ideas about whether Keynes was right and restrict myself to the role of a translator. It soon transpired that, taken past a point, this agnostic approach led to a woodenness of style; and even the organization of my book implicitly drew on a set of values. Yet it has been my ideal, and I have tried to explain Keynes's ideas rather than my own.

Subject to all of the above limitations, I have tried to write as directly as possible. There are many side roads which I have not explored, and questions about the accuracy of Keynes's own commentaries on other authors which I have not raised. I have not tried to develop any subject except as it has contributed to my theme, and many scholars who might otherwise expect to be honoured in a work of this nature have not been mentioned. Others have been criticized over some point that they might regard as inessential, and the overall value of their work has not been considered.

Among those whom I must thank I mention first my former student Michael Browne, both for his intellectual companionship and because his thesis, concerning the impact of G. E. Moore on Keynes, influenced this book. I thank Robert Skidelsky, who encouraged me when he did not entirely agree with my ideas, and who pointed to a flaw in the original work. Victoria Chick helped more than she could know; what had seemed my outlandish heresy became more commonplace after it was proclaimed to her under the high heavens of Hampstead Heath. Bruce Littleboy read my manuscript and convinced me that the macroeconomics should be reworked—perhaps he will still think so. Rosanne Fitzgibbons assisted on points of style, and Olwen Schubert gave good humoured co-operation though she had to type innumerable changes to the draft of this book. I should also mention my macroeconomics class ten years ago at the University of Queensland, when I began to recognize the pre-modern element in Keynes. That class was also taught political philosophy by Dick Staveley, and some of my early ideas were stimulated by his.

Finally I would like to thank the Royal Economic Society for permission to quote extensively from Keynes's *Collected Writings*. I am also grateful to King's College at Cambridge for permission to draw on the unpublished writings of Keynes, and to Michael Hall, who guided me through the Keynes library in King's College.

Contents

1

Introduction

It is hardly an exaggeration to say that customary standards
of interpretation have been less consistently employed in the
analysis of Keynes' contribution than in assessing the
accomplishment of any other major economist.

Axel Leijonhufvud, *On Keynesian Economics
and the Economics of Keynes*

In what follows I will show that it is possible to draw from the
writings of John Maynard Keynes, without artificiality, a
logically coherent and embracing structure of ideas, based upon
a single vision, which permeated all aspects of his thought and
which, except for one major and identifiable change, was
constant through time. This structure of ideas includes Keynes's
theories of probability and uncertainty, and his unsuspected but
well defined philosophies of morals and politics. It also underlies
the new economic method in the *General Theory of Money, Interest
and Employment*, which was Keynes's greatest work.

I am concerned here not with the merit of Keynes's economic
policies, important though they are, but, according to a
distinction made by Keynes after he wrote the *General Theory*,
with the ideas underlying those policies:

I am more attached to the comparatively simple fundamental ideas
which underlie my theory than to the particular forms in which I have
embodied them, and I have no desire that the latter should be
crystallized at the present stage of the debate. (XIV: 111)[1]

Since Keynes wrote these words, economists have crystallized
the particular forms of his ideas and have often found them
wanting, but they have not much addressed the 'comparatively
simple' underlying concepts.

Keynes's system was consciously cast as a third alternative to both Marxism and *laissez-faire*, and it is the only comprehensive alternative which says that the economy is neither a perfect machine nor a system doomed to failure, but a fallible human institution improvable by human reason. Yet, although in the past his theories regulated the major economies of the world, Keynes's ringing word-spells have slowly lost their power. His followers have often adopted, as though it were a virtue, an intellectual superficiality which has subverted their own doctrine. They remained silent when his theories were judged on the basis of a method alien to his own; Keynesianism without Keynes has come to seem unpolitical, unevocative and narrow, whereas Marxism and *laissez-faire* draw their economic theories from a wider set of ideas. Yet Keynes did not himself put morals and economics in separate compartments of the soul, and he formulated his third way in terms that were wide and comprehensive. He declared economics to be a method rather than a set of theories, and he regarded his own method as superior because it alone followed a philosophy of practical action. He believed that Marxism and *laissez-faire* shared a method that was too abstract to capture probabilistic reality and too materialistic to reflect rational values.

Of course, there are many conflicting interpretations of Keynes. There is Joan Robinson's Keynes, who delivered the funeral ovation for *laissez-faire*, and T. W. Hutchison's Keynes, who defended *laissez-faire*. There is R. F. Harrod's Keynes, whose goals were truth, unworldiness and other absolute values, and Robert Skidelsky's Keynes, who was on his way to a party via Marx and Freud. There is Don Patinkin's Keynes, who admired mathematical economics, and Paul Davidson's Keynes, who overthrew general equilibrium theory. The Keynes the public knows stands for big government, whereas F. von Hayek's Keynes wanted government to be small. Philosophers know Keynes as the modern founder of the logical theory of probability, whereas G. L. S. Shackle has taught economists to regard him as the founder of the subjective theory of probability, which is the opposite.

Arguments about Keynes's central message have constituted a doctrinal fog, but only recently have economists begun to study his *Treatise on Probability*, while his moral and political philosophies remain largely unknown. In addition, 'Keynesian' economics often bears little relation to the original, so that there does not seem to be a single work, for example, that seriously considers Keynes's definition of value, despite his claims to have made an innovation in this area. It is hoped that economists will eventually follow the example of those astronomers who, at first regarding the study of cosmological origins as speculative and unscientific, later found that it was one of the focal points of their subject.

I will draw on these overlooked and neglected elements to show that Keynes's innovation was to reconcile economics with the older traditions of moral and political philosophy. The difficulty of understanding even the technical aspects of his economics arises because we have long been divorced from that tradition. Its last representative in England was Edmund Burke, and he was archaic, a contemporary and admirer of Adam Smith, but in no way possessing Smith's intuitions of economic progress. Today we breathe a different intellectual air, and our modern assumptions are hidden from ourselves.

Keynes's vision was a metaphysical idea by which he effected this reconciliation of the old and the new. It was partly enunciated by his biographer Robert Skidelsky, not when he said that the secret lay in Keynes's personal life, but when, faced with a problem of how much to reveal, he said that he would follow Keynes and adopt ruthless truth-telling regardless of the consequences. I will show below that truth as a foundation for action was as fundamental to Keynes as the relativity of values is fundamental to modern economics.

From his pre-modern vision came Keynes's theory of probability, which explained the world as a flux of affairs that is partly, but only partly, revealed. There also came Keynes's ethics, which differentiated not between science and values, but between what is rational and what is not, and could include ethics in the rational. It led to Keynes's political philosophy, which he devised by replacing the religious conventions in Burke with his own vision, while keeping the structure of Burke's system.

These general ideas in turn led to Keynes's practical methods and the context of his specific theories. Keynes's pragmatism is not a personal peccadillo but an aspect of his political philosophy; the 'moral science' of economics referred to in the *General Theory* was an application of this political philosophy to the economic sphere. His theory of uncertainty is an interplay between probability, ethics and the economic flux; and his theories of value and interest in the *General Theory* are meant to express the flux formally.

To support this interpretation of Keynes, I have drawn upon some of his early unpublished writings. However, I am not adding to the many existing accounts of Keynes, but am presenting a new interpretation that, it is hoped, will change our understanding of him. Keynes's economics is about uncertainty, but the interpretation of the neo-Keynesian economists remains closer to that of the neo-classical economists than either is to my interpretation. In many respects these schools are traditional enemies, but they both interpret Keynes as a materialist, whereas I agree with Keynes's own statement that he was on the left wing of celestial space.

The philosophy that everywhere prevails in modern economics has so distorted perceptions of Keynes that the philosophy in which he set his economic theories has been virtually disregarded; and if this disregard has arisen from antipathy or wilful incomprehension, it would even be accurate to say that Keynes's philosophy has been suppressed. Despite all the interpretations, Keynes's political economy has not been systematically analysed as a system in its own right. Comments on it tend to be *obiter dicta*, the primary intent of which has been not to explain his views but to advance some other system. Although there are political antagonisms among economists, they generally share a materialist world view which Keynes rejected. Therefore a systematically biased interpretation of the *General Theory* has developed, and this bias has omitted key elements of Keynesian philosophy which may be of particular relevance today.

This distortion of Keynes's ideas occurred more readily because Keynes was not an explicit systematizer, and his deeper observations were scattered among his works, many of which are written in a technical vein for economists. Despite this, Keynes's influence upon the thought and politics of the twentieth century has been comparable to that of Marx; and the prospects for capitalism may yet depend upon whether its economics and politics will only express class and vested interests, as Marx believed, or whether Keynes was more to the point in the pursuit of 'new truths which might alter the course of events'.

It is now known that for about thirty years formalistic 'Keynesian' economics dominated the economics literature with technical constructs or assumptions that were gratuitously attributed to Keynes, but were not his at all. However, it has not been recognized that there are critical elements in the interpretation of Keynes that have simply been omitted because they are too anomalous. In short, scholarship has recognized the attribution of views to Keynes but not the systematic subtraction from his ideas. I believe that many omitted elements, such as Keynes's declaration that he was a pre-classical economist, his monetary theory of interest, his philosophy of objective chance, his belief in natural law and his neo-Platonic religion, are fundamental. They form a new and unified and fascinating theme, essential to the understanding of his economics, when Keynes is interpreted according to his own lights.

Debates about what Keynes said or meant tend to refer to his views concerning capitalism, or to the assumptions in his technical economics. However, these debates cannot be resolved independently of issues that were more fundamental to Keynes. His economics has not been adequately recognized as an expression of his probabilistic and moral philosophies. These are the implicit and inseparable foundations of Keynes's economic policies, despite their unpalatability to many economists. The desire of economists to adopt Keynes's policies while disregarding their intellectual origin may have had the most detrimental economic and political consequences; for, regardless to whether they accept or reject his policies, economists have been operating under a misconception.

Notes to Chapter 1

1. XIV:111 refers to Vol. XIV, p. 111 of the *Collected Writings of John Maynard Keynes*. I have followed this notation unless referring to the *General Theory* (*GT*), which is well known by that name rather than as Vol. VII of the *Collected Writings*. With the exception of Keynes's long essay, 'The Political Principles of Edmund Burke', it is not possible to paginate references to the early writings.

PART I

Philosophy

2

Probability

One may truly say, that there are very few lovers of truth for truth's sake, even amongst those who persuade themselves that they are so. How a man may know whether he be so in earnest, is worth inquiry: and I think there is one unerring mark of it, viz., the not entertaining any proposition with greater assurance, than the proofs it is built upon will warrant. Whoever goes beyond this measure of assent, it is plain, receives not truth in the love of it; loves not truth for truth's sake, but for some other by-end.

John Locke, *An Essay Concerning Human Understanding*

In the chapters that follow, it will become evident that Keynes's economic and political philosophy can be understood only as a reversion to pre-modernity, that Keynes analysed the modern economy by means of a pre-modern philosophy. He held that there is an irregularity and transience in practical affairs which thwarts the methods of science and obliges the decision-maker to rely upon intuition; and although Keynes recognized that intuition was fallible, he believed that it could nevertheless operate according to logic by drawing, through analogies, upon models that were not necessarily in the world but were understood in the mind.

The *Treatise on Probability*, which is Keynes's most formal statement of this pre-modern philosophy, lists the major influences upon him. The earliest English influence cited was John Locke, supporter of Charles I and author of *An Essay Concerning Human Understanding*, a philosopher between the medieval schoolmen and the moderns. Keynes drew from Locke a medieval distinction between the atomic substratum that constitutes the invisible machinery of the world, and the secondary characteristics or attributes by which we understand it. However, he did not agree with Locke that truth is known only through experience of the world.

From David Hume, author of *A Treatise of Human Nature*, contemporary of Adam Smith and prototype of the modern scientific positivist, Keynes learned that there is the same structure in the logic of probability and the logic of ethics. However, he rejected Hume's scepticism towards probability and ethics and also his religion of theoretical science.

From G. E. Moore, Keynes's own mentor at Cambridge, author of *Principia Ethica* and an antagonist of Hume, Keynes learned that the intuition grasps not just the facts of the world but also the ultimate and ideal. However, he did not agree with Moore that the ideal was unrelated to questions about action.

Out of the obscure fragments and incantations of these and other philosophers, Keynes wove a magical carpet which took him both backwards and forwards in intellectual time. This chapter shows what it meant when Keynes rejected Hume in favour of Locke's theory of causation, and how, by rejecting Locke's empiricism, Keynes passed back to pre-modernity. Later we will see that he found pre-modern philosophy to be wanting only because it did not take account of economic growth. I have suggested that it is the unpalatability of Keynes's pre-modern philosophy that makes his economics so difficult to assimilate. Keynes's intention in the *Treatise on Probability*, wrote J. J. Klant (1985: 83), 'was to solve the induction problem which had been set by David Hume'.[1] More generally, Keynes's philosophy can be understood as a wide-ranging series of attacks on Hume's philosophy, for Hume was at the critical pass where science challenged metaphysics for pre-eminence. Keynes would later declare that economics was not a natural science, which implied that he thought the pass was retaken.

The Principle of Indifference

Keynes's *Treatise on Probability* can be delineated by two earlier works that came out of Cambridge. *The Principia Mathematica* by Russell and Whitehead laid down the axiomatic basis of mathematics, while G. E. Moore's *Principia Ethica* meant to lay down the logical foundations of ethics. The ambit of probability intrudes into the two principiae, which means into logical deduction and moral philosophy. It applies directly to the whole field of empirical thinking. Probability applies to gambling and games, but it also applies to statistics, economics, politics and law, scientific induction and the ordinary conduct of life, which as the truism says is never certain. Keynes's argument was that in most cases, many more than had been recognized, the probability of an event could be determined only by an act of judgement.

Keynes criticized the superficialities of the school of mathematical probability, because the mathematicians tended to disregard the meaning of their assumptions in order to proceed with their calculations. The 'incautious methods and exaggerated claims of the school of Laplace' had arrived at 'complicated results of the greatest precision and the most profound practical importance' (VIII:55), without knowing their own axiomatic foundations. In particular, they indiscriminantly assumed and built upon what Keynes called the 'principle of indifference', which is that in a state of ignorance we can attach 50 per cent to the probability of an event occurring and 50 per cent to it not occurring. Keynes argued that beyond a narrow and limited scope, such as in a game of chance, the principle of indifference is facile and logically inconsistent.

The *General Theory*, written about two decades later, denounces the principle of indifference without actually naming it. With respect to the calculation of investment returns under conditions of uncertainty, Keynes wrote, 'It can easily be shown that the assumption of arithmetically equal probabilities based on a state of ignorance leads to absurdities' (*GT*:152). In a state of ignorance it is illegitimate to assume that an event has a 50 per cent chance of occurring; if I assume in a state of ignorance that the next car I see is 50 per cent likely to be blue, then the same method extended to other colours will drive me to a self-contradiction. Keynes believed that the principle of indifference is not often applicable, and that it can be validly assumed only when there is *positive* reason, in an otherwise state of ignorance, to believe the odds are equal and there is only white statistical noise in the background. For example, he ridiculed the principle by quoting the following exchange, in which both parties are drawing on the principle of indifference in an equally facile way to reach contradictory conclusions:

Absolute: 'Sure, Sir, this is not very reasonable, to summon my affection for a lady I know nothing of.'

Sir Anthony: 'I am sure, Sir, 'tis more unreasonable in you to object to a lady you know nothing of.'

(Quoted in VIII:44)

For the most part, the world is too complex to be explained by a theory that applies to the tossing of a coin.

This, we will see, is why Keynes had particular reservations about econometrics. However, Keynes did not regard his criticism of the methods of the School of Laplace as fundamental. It was his disagreement with Hume that he declared to be more fundamental (VIII:55), but the force of his attack on Hume was obscured by the superficialities of the statisticians. Hume's theory was that *all* probable knowledge was invalid, and that only knowledge contained in mathematical and logical theories was valid. Keynes believed that to escape Hume's scepticism the statisticians had invalidly dressed probable knowledge in mathematical terms, to make probability look like science. Their error had to be exposed in order to attend to the real issue, which was the valid status of probable knowledge in the general, non-quantifiable, sense.

The algebraical exercises, in which the Chevalier de la Méré interested Pascal, have so far predominated in the learned world over the profounder enquiries of the philosopher into those processes of human faculty which, by determining reasonable preference, guide our choice, that Probability is oftener reckoned with Mathematics than with Logic. (VIII:Preface)

Keynes believed that most probabilities were unquantifiable. If the weather looks like rain but the forecast says clear, we normally cannot meaningfully determine the chances of rain. The reinsurance rate for a vessel lost off South Africa fluctuated wildly after each rumour or irrelevant recollection, no correct rate being conceivable. 'It is not the case here that the method of calculation, prescribed by theory, is beyond our powers or is too laborious for actual application. *No* method of calculation however impracticable, has been suggested' (VIII:32).

Even apart from uncertainty, there are various probabilities that are not commensurable, as when they apply to different contributory causes of an event. We cannot combine the statistical chance of winning a beauty contest with the probabilities pertaining to the personal taste of the judge. It may not be meaningful to put a numerical figure on the probability of an event, as when we consider the likelihood that a certain picture was painted by a particular painter, or the extent to which another successful test of a scientific theory supports confidence in the theory. Mathematical probability has a role to play, but its scope has been greatly exaggerated by unwarranted applications of the principle of indifference.

Keynes stressed unquantifiable probabilities not in order to show the difficulty of making a reasonable judgement, but more to show the power of the mind. He believed that the mind contains a faculty of direct judgement, which to some extent is aware of, and can apply, the principles required to reach a probabilistic conclusion. 'There is little likelihood of our discovering a method of recognizing particular probabilities, without any assistance whatever from intuition or direct judgement.' Nevertheless, these judgements may be controlled by logical rules and principles. 'The fact that we ultimately depend upon an intuition need not lead us to suppose that our conclusions have, therefore, no basis in reason, or that they are as subjective in validity as they are in origin' (VIII:76).

As an indication of this faculty of mind, Keynes mentioned the close analogy between probability and similarity, it being generally accepted that we can say objectively whether things are similar to one another. In some cases it is possible to quantify similarity, as when things differ only by size or weight; but usually similar things differ in a variety of respects, and then some overall judgement must be made as to the degree of similarity between them. This cannot be done conclusively, but it still can be done, because the mind does in fact judge degrees of similarity. However, 'one argument is more probable than another (i.e. nearer to certainty) in the same kind of way as we can describe one object as more like another to a standard object of comparison' (VIII:39). As similarity is to identity, so is probability to logical inference. Keynes's argument was that, just as a judgement concerning similarity seeks to base itself on some intuitive but real ground, so too does a judgement concerning probability. In each case, the mind works from an intuition that experience suggests is rational.

The *Treatise* criticizes the frequency theory of probability, which says a probability can be known only after the event and never before it. The theory in the *Treatise* is known as the *logical theory of probability*, so distinguishing it from those theories (the modern versions arising in reaction against Keynes's *Treatise*) that argue that all judgement is essentially capricious or meaningless. The logical approach means that probability relations are a branch of logical relations, an idea that Keynes seems to have conceived as an extension of the methods of *Principia Mathematica*. It means that, just as there is a deductive logic which deals with the categories of correct and false deduction, so too there is a larger logic which deals with the categories of knowledge, ignorance and rational belief. This logic of probability is concerned not with the subjective, but with the objective grounds for belief.

'A proposition is not probable because we think it so' (VIII:4). For example, the evidence suggests that there are reasonable grounds, independent of the idiosyncrasies of the observer, for preferring the Darwinian theory of evolution. Evolution theory has not been conclusively proved, but the evidence suggests a justified degree of belief. Keynes admitted that the evidence available concerning each theory is often different for different persons, but there is nevertheless an objective belief, which a rational person would recognize, associated with his available evidence.

All this is reasonably consistent with common sense, and we usually think we exercise some sort of 'logical intuition' when we consider whether to take an umbrella if it looks like rain. There are strong evolutionary reasons why people should somehow develop faculties to assess a future situation, as Keynes noted in a single brief comment on the *Treatise* years later. However, the field of probability extends beyond common sense, and rational intuition has important implications for scientific method which are not so generally acceptable. Scientists are supposed to hold scientific theories not as probably true, but only as tentative, and until there is contrary evidence. More importantly, intuition and judgement are epiphenomenal and beyond direct scientific analysis. The logical theory of probability therefore represented a challenge to the primacy of scientific method and scientific knowledge.

Disagreement with Hume

Keynes supported a common-sense interpretation of probability instead of the strict 'scientific' interpretation. He took issue with Hume, who had understood probability in as wide a sense as Keynes, but had argued that there could be no logical sense in a probability judgement. Hume has been the master concerning probability and scientific induction, wrote Keynes. Far from believing that the mind is capable of logical intuitions, Hume believed that it was capable of logic only in respect to mathematical and logical tautologies; for the rest, he described the mind as being subject to a flow of sensations of 'inconceivable rapidity, and in perpetual flux and movement', and concluded that any judgement, be it a judgement of values or of probabilities, could only be based upon conventions, operating through the imagination.

There are diametric differences between Keynes and Hume over probability, the theory of causation, the theory of the mind, the philosophy of scientific method, the relevance of beauty and the philosophy of action. Also, in the *End of Laissez-Faire*, Keynes says that Hume is the real originator of utilitarianism, the ethics which he believed underlay conventional economics and which he regarded as a shallow rival to his own ethics. In each of these areas Hume meant to show that the role of reason was much more restricted than had been understood. Keynes, to the contrary, wanted to show that reason has a greater role; but to do this he had to adopt a dualistic theory, to show the spheres of both reason and unreason and to connect them. The connection, which was only completed in the *General Theory*, was through the theory of probability and uncertainty. Keynes's position was modified over time, in a way that he described in general terms, but his opposition to Humian thinking was consistent.

Hume was the original formulator of the distinction between the positive and the normative, or the strict division between statements that say what 'is' and statements that say what 'ought to be'. According to Hume, factual statements constitute knowledge, whereas moral statements are based only upon the imagination. ''Tis not contrary to reason', he wrote, 'to prefer the destruction of the whole world to the scratching of my finger'—a sentiment that Keynes described as 'cynical' (IX:274). Because probability statements lack rigour, Hume believed that such statements were akin to moral arguments, both being based on the imagination; and so 'all probable reasoning is but a species of sensation'.[2]

Keynes agreed with Hume that judgements of probability and judgements of value had the same status, but he believed that both could be valid. 'The importance of probability', he wrote in the *Treatise on Probability*, 'is that it is *rational* to be guided by it in action . . . that in action we *ought* to take some account of it' (VIII:356).

Hume thought that the man of action cannot express truth, as the philosopher does, because to survive in the world a man of action needs to wrongly represent to himself that his (merely probable) worldly knowledge has some real basis. But even the philosopher needs to live in the world sometimes. Evidently the philosopher (for whom today we might read the scientist) must oscillate between his studies, where he is a sceptic, and his everyday life, where he must rely on unfounded beliefs, because when he is active in the world he is divorced from his principles. To put Hume's argument into modern terms, unless the scientist abandons his professional scepticism and accepts that the trains will *probably* run, he will never get to work. He may refuse to define an attitude to probabilistic knowledge when he is in the laboratory, but he has no choice when he is trying to get there.

Keynes rejected Hume's divorce between truth and action because Keynes believed that a logical method should be expressed and embodied in action. Hume speaks at points of the façade that the philosopher presents because he cannot be altogether divorced from ordinary life.

Most fortunately it happens that since reason is incapable of dispelling these clouds [of scepticism], Nature herself suffices to that purpose . . . I find myself absolutely and necessarily determined to live, and talk and act like other people in the common affairs of life. (*Treatise of Human Nature*, Bk. I, Pt. 4, Sect. 7)

Keynes believed that an alternation of mind was characteristic of Hume. There was no need, he said, for Hume to have fancied himself some 'strange uncouth monster, who not being able to mingle and unite in society, had been expell'd all human commerce, and left utterly abandon'd and disconsolate'. The difficulty simply was that Hume's scepticism 'goes too far' (VIII:55).

Keynes agreed with Hume that practical men must act on probabilistic knowledge, but Hume had further believed that a truth-seeking philosopher could not also be practical. Although Keynes has been criticized because his *Treatise* does not take us far 'if we are trying to find out what scientists do or ought to do', that was by no means his intention. It would be much closer to say that Keynes meant to determine what men of action do and ought to do, a matter Keynes pursued over a lifetime beginning with the *Treatise on Probability*. In a draft preface to the *Treatise*, he wrote: 'The logic of probability is of the greatest importance, because it is the logic of ordinary discourse, through which the practical conclusions of action are most often reached.' The difficulty was that to develop a rational philosophy of action he had to depart from an over-proud philosophy of science. Later, to anticipate our story, Keynes would depart from economic science and develop a method that recognized probability and the need for rational action.

Hume's scepticism went too far because he believed that under conditions of probability, which is the usual state of knowledge, causation has no objective meaning except in theory. 'Objects have no discoverable connection together', according to Hume, because strict logic does not apply to probability. So causation is between propositions (as in a scientific theory) and not in reality, or in relations between *things*. It is a defence of abstract theory, to the effect that we never know what is really happening in the buzzing blooming world but only what our theory says is happening. In particular, it could also be regarded as a model for the abstract economic theory of David Ricardo, whose method was criticized by Keynes.

Keynes reverted to Locke's theory, which gave two meanings of causation that he believed Hume had confused. According to one of these meanings, objects have no *strict* connection together, although there is a partial connection which is sometimes discoverable; according to the other meaning, objects do have a strict connection together, but normally this is not discoverable. We do not know *real* causes, but only probabilities. Keynes's philosophy of causation is the foundation of much of his *Treatise on Probability*, including his theories of probability and judgement. In a brilliant essay, Anna Carabelli has pointed to the significance of Keynes's distinction between the medieval terms *causa essendi*, the explanation of the atomic constitution of the universe, and *causa cognoscendi*, the scientific laws and common knowledge of the universe (Carabelli 1985a:153–4). Keynes believed that, except in a few sciences, we do not normally understand the true causes of things but only the causes *cognoscendi*, or what is a cause according to our theories, which is strictly not a cause at all.

Ground or Reason is that upon which a judgment is based as an act of thought. Every relation of causation is a ground. Still there is a difference of aspect between Ground and Cause; the latter is the *causa essendi*, the cause of why a thing is what it is; the former is the *causa cognoscendi*—the cause of our knowledge of the event. A statement of a law may be a Ground, never a Cause, though the law may involve causal relations, and lay down what causes are followed by what effects. (Quoted in Carabelli 1985a:154)

Causa essendi is cause in the strict sense, but *causa cognoscendi* is the term that applies in the everyday surface world, where events are far too complex to be understood in terms of the atomic units. In this surface world, knowledge is made up of loose classifications which are not bound by rules of constant behaviour. Because of his activist philosophy, Keynes's interest lay not in *causa essendi* but in *causa cognoscendi*—'I have nothing useful to say about them [causal laws]. Nearly everything with which I deal can be expressed in terms of logical relevance', he wrote, adding that there is only a 'doubtful' relation between 'logical relevance' and material cause.

The Atomic Flux

Keynes accepted Locke's view that the physical universe is atomic, which means that the universe consists of the collision and arrangement of small particles which are themselves limited in variety. Atomism also applies at the human level, because in principle the biologists explain human qualities by the collision and arrangements of the chromosomes. Atomism, or the hypothesis that there is a limited variety of atomic particles, leads us to believe that there are certain regularities in the universe, or at least that there is not an infinite number of possibilities. The limited variety of atoms in the universe is a precondition for there being similarities between things, and so it is possible to draw up classifications based on similarities between them.

However, Keynes's argument proceeds, it has not been understood how subtle and hidden the ultimate atomic characters are. In addition, goodness is not atomic, but complex or organic, meaning that we do not want particular arrangements of atoms to occur, but evaluate each set of circumstances in overall terms. Only some of the physical sciences can follow a method of causal exactitude, or analyse in terms of fundamental atomic units. It is because of the more usual human inability to think in genuinely causal atomic terms, and the normal irrelevance anyway of these terms, that we live in a probabilistic world. Probability and uncertainty must be understood in reference to human minds and not in reference to super-minds which could hypothetically see the workings of the causal substratum. Probability is 'relative in a sense to the principles of *human* reason' (VIII:35). Because human minds cannot decipher the atomic buzz, we must recognize that our theories will not be truly causal but only probable and generalist accounts, so that for example counter-instances need not necessarily refute these theories.

Yet, although we are unaware of the true causal chain, some knowledge is still possible, ultimately because the mind is to some extent aware of certain principles which describe the universe, and because analogies can be drawn from these principles.[3] Because the mind sees murkily, these principles are not exactly true as we understand them, and experience may refute them, as perhaps Einstein's theory of relativity may contradict the uniformity of nature. In the end, however, we do not have any other means of knowledge, because if knowledge is traced back it will be found to be inextricably dependent upon principles of varying generality. Knowledge depends upon principles that are imperfectly understood because they begin as patterns in the mind.

We cannot rely on observation by itself. Keynes agreed with Hume that the mere counting of identical instances could not support a theory. If the instances were genuinely identical, then one hundred supporting observations of a theory can tell us no more than one. However, Keynes did not agree with Hume and J. S. Mill that knowledge is more advanced by the refutation of general laws than by the compilation of evidence in their favour. He said that Mill and Hume failed to recognize that the habits of nature are general tendencies rather than invariable, the possible contingencies being too numerous to be covered by a finite number of experiments. When we recognize that knowledge is only probabilistic, we must also acknowledge that we do not ever know when all the relevant circumstances of two scientific tests are genuinely identical, which means that we never know for certain that a general law has been refuted. To show that a law holds under some circumstances and not under others is an advance of knowledge, but each set of circumstances is in some ways different from each other set. (If ever the circumstances were identical, we would never know it.) Yet to determine whether there are any *essential* differences between the circumstances under which a theory is tested, we are again dependent upon a judgement of similarity. Consequently, judgement underlies all knowledge.

These differences between the circumstances of a test Keynes called their 'negative analogy'; the relation between the hypothesis and the conclusions, which is never perfect in actuality, he called the 'positive analogy'. The general point is that nearly everything we know is based upon analogy and similarity. Induction by itself, the mere counting of instances, does not tell us anything, and only induction that supports a theory advances knowledge. Yet any theory must be based upon analogy if it is to say anything about the real world. All knowledge depends ultimately upon analogy with what we already know, and so upon principles of knowledge seen only murkily by the mind. Science is more limited than we understand, and it does not lead to any absolute truths. That a scientific investigation, pursued on account of its probability, will generally lead to truth is at the best only probable. 'There is no direct relation between the truth of a proposition and its probability. Probability begins and ends with probability' (VIII:356). Keynes did not oppose his philosophy of probability to his commitment to truth, but his moral is that scientific knowledge is as limited as any other form of knowledge. There are processes in a causal web beyond our sciences or powers of calculation. If we stamp our feet, Keynes says, the moons of Jupiter may be slightly displaced in their orbits, although our sciences are not fine enough to recognize it. As small effects may have large consequences, judgement must determine which strands in the causal web should come to the attention of science. But if we knew everything that human minds could know, there would still be probability and uncertainty arising from our inherent limitations. 'We must consider the knowledge which is relative not to actual knowledge but to a certain kind of knowledge', the knowledge that it is feasible for us to know. We must not implicitly assume that we have superhuman minds. The complexity of things makes science limited and partial.

Although the universe considered abstractly may be atomic—and at the end Keynes wonders whether the atomic constitution is artificially forced upon it by the scientific mind—knowledge of the universe is evidently organic. More fully, and bearing in mind G. E. Moore's theories, we may understand Keynes to say that the universe, together with our consciousness of it, conjointly forms an organic whole.

Precise mathematical methods are appropriate for unravelling the *causa essendi*, because they proceed on the assumption that there are calculable and limited effects between defined bodies. But if knowledge is organic, then the rules of understanding are changed; mechanistic methods will be defeated by subtle and complex feedback effects, and if the theory tries to abstract from them by means of partial analysis, then the more significant part of the story will always be left out of account.

If knowledge is organic, there are not even rules against logical contradiction, because categories cannot have constant or even definable meanings. The emphasis must be on the spirit of what is said, and not on what Keynes elsewhere called 'logical nitpickings'. His method, wrote G. L. S. Shackle, was no reliance on tool box theory, but 'reliance on the mysterious and fathomless power of words' (Shackle 1974:75). It is like a logic of colours, said Carabelli (1985a). She also called it a logic of common discourse (p. 165), but the emphasis should be put on 'discourse' rather than on 'common', the point being that *causa cognoscendi* is understood only through analogy, and that language contains the most evocative metaphors. Organic unities require a logic of metaphoric understanding, which is not surprising, given that Moore drew upon organic unities mainly to illustrate the nature of beauty.

Objective Chance

The principle of indifference invalidly tries to impose a pattern on the atomic chaos, and Keynes responded with the opposite idea of objective chance. Objective chance prevails when prediction is impossible in principle, given our human limitations. Objective chance covers such things as the distribution of raindrops, the motion of gas molecules, the birth of a great man, the shuffling of cards and errors of observation. It does not arise out of limitations within our normal powers of observation, or out of scepticism about common sense. 'An event is not due to objective chance if a knowledge of the permanent facts of existence would lead to its prediction.' We approach it through an inherent human mediocrity.

An event is due to objective chance if in order to predict it, or to prefer it to alternatives . . . it would be necessary to know a great many more facts of existence about it than we actually do know, and if the addition of a wide knowledge of general principles would be little use. (VIII:319)

The permanent facts of existence included whatever was known and outside erratic chance, and so it bracketed together reliable conventions with scientific laws.[4] Keynes believed that the idea of objective chance had not been understood by those who wanted to argue that there is an equilibrium value in randomness, who wished to rely on constant statistical frequencies or the Law of Great Numbers, who stressed what will happen 'in the long run', who believed that there is a unique discoverable system among the chance and disorder of the universe. The precise and stringent conditions for the operation of the Law of Great Numbers almost never hold: 'Our so-called permanent causes are always changing a little and are liable at any moment to radical alteration', he wrote, foreshadowing his idea of uncertainty in the *General Theory*.

The name Keynes gave to objective chance is misleading; objective chance is not the opposite to subjective chance, but is the opposite to the causal theory, which is implicit in the Laplacian way of understanding things. Keynes drew upon the French mathematician Henri Poincaré. 'We certainly do not use the term "chance"', he quoted Poincaré as saying, 'as the ancients used it, in opposition to determinism.' The confusion is greater because Keynes overlooked a tradition that would have made his difficult concept more full and clear. Objective chance is really an independent rediscovery of the Greek notion of necessity, and Keynes and Poincaré notwithstanding, the Greeks expressly did mean to reconcile determinism and chance. Indeed, a reference to the ideas of these ancients might clarify Keynes's own version of objective chance.

Necessity as the errant or wandering cause has been analysed at length by F. M. Cornford, who shows that for the Greeks 'the idea of necessity is opposed to purpose and linked with spontaneity, coincidence and chance'. Necessity was the 'indeterminate, the inconstant, the anomalous, which can neither be understood nor predicted', according to the classical scholar Grote; or (Professor Cornford again) it is 'force, movement or change with the negative attribute of not being regular, or intelligible, or determined by any knowable antecedent or condition'.[5] In short, it is the subject of the *causa essendi*, the patternless whizzing atoms in the invisible atomic substratum, causation without order.

We may contrast objective chance with games of pure chance. Objective chance is manifested by the conjunction of unrelated probabilistic series, and Keynes gives as an example a man who is walking down a street and is hit by a tile. There is no implication that the various probabilities in objective chance have to be quantifiable, and to apply objective chance to a dice game, we would perhaps have to combine it with another game or let the players cheat in unsuspected ways. Keynes criticized the School of Laplace because he did not think that pure games had much relevance to the real world, and objective chance fills the gap. It appears undeclared in the background of most of Keynes's economic theories, because objective chance is simply what manifests when long-run equilibrium thinking does not apply. It is the conceptual alternative to long-run thinking. More than that, the very concept of the errant or wandering cause arises out of a deep scepticism towards the pre-eminence of scientific method. As Cornford said, it is not the ancients but the *moderns* who connect necessity with intelligible order and regular sequence, the aim of modern science being to formulate laws of regular causation. Keynes connected true causation with randomness, a way of thinking that had the utmost significance for his economics.

The Great War was to be an intellectual watershed which brought home to Keynes the force of human irrationality, but in the *Treatise on Probability*, which was mostly written before 1914, an oversimplified rationalism is in full flood. Keynes believed that the flux, which Hume had thought was in the mind, was in the universe outside, at least as humans can know it. 'One could say the same thing . . . about most things, for the consequences, even if they persist, are generally lost in the river of time' (X:55). Although the only universe we can ever know is an ever changing stream, the mind remains capable of rational intuitions which can faintly discern beyond the flow and through turbulent airs the transcosmic ideals. Humanity lives in a 'twilight of probability', but it sees lights through the fog.

Creativity and the Veil of Partial Ignorance

The logical theory of probability presupposes intuition, and although it does not require that intuition is infallible or even mostly right, the stress is as much on insight as it is on theory. Logically as well as historically, according to Keynes, intuition is the first form of knowledge, so that despite its defects all knowledge must be based upon it. However, he did not suppose that intuition came out of nowhere. Probabilistic reasoning meant being able to apply patterns of similarity, first seen in the mind, to the chaotic facts. 'Keynes thought that science did possess procedures similar to those of art', writes Carabelli, referring to Keynes's early paper on beauty; and she adds, 'The role of creativity and intuition in science was analogous to that played in the appreciation of beauty' (Carabelli: 1985b:158).

In his *Theory on Beauty*, Keynes noted that Hume regarded science and art as separate. We can either discover the most secret springs and principles of something, or else describe the grace and beauty of its action. 'I imagine it impossible', he quoted Hume as saying, 'to combine these two views.' But Keynes did combine them, saying that the only difference was that the scientists spent more time mixing the paints. The 'mechanical theory of the external world', a supposed unique correspondence between the facts and the mind, was false. Inspiration selects and imposes a pattern on the facts, and the choice of this pattern somehow involves an aesthetic element.

This picture of the scientist as partly an artist was further taken up in the *Treatise on Probability*, where Keynes said that science begins from analogy. Science is based upon pre-scientific knowledge, which was long and hard won; and scientific hypotheses do not arise randomly, but they too come from analogy. If those analogies are often wrong, they are none the less not foolish, for they are the origins of our knowledge. For example, religious systems from Pythagoras to Comte have sought to derive strength from the virtue of the number seven, and even Newton was misled by the analogy between the seven tones of music and the seven colours of the spectrum. Yet it would be rash to say that in the hands of Pythagoras the special virtue of the number seven would only coincidentally lead to success:

Is it certain that Newton and Huyghens were only reasonable when their theories were true, and that their mistakes were the fruit of a disordered fancy? Or that the savages, from whom we have inherited the most fundamental inductions of our knowledge, were always superstitious when they believed what we now know to be preposterous?' (VIII:274)

One of the last things Keynes wrote was a biography of Isaac Newton, whom he presented as the epitome of intellectual intuition. 'So happy in his conjectures,' Keynes quoted a contemporary as saying, 'as to seem to know more than he could possibly have any means of proving.' Until Keynes's biography, Newton had commonly been regarded as a mechanist, and since the days of Hume the social sciences have been urged to follow the mechanistic method that is supposed to underlie Newton's physics. Keynes's portrait of Newton counterpoised Newton's scientific work against his magical and creative genius.

Newton was not the first of the age of reason. He was the last of the magicians, the last of the Babylonians and Sumerians, the last great mind which looked out on the visible and intellectual world with the same eyes as those who began to build our intellectual inheritance rather less than 10,000 years ago. (X:364)

Newton travelled strange seas of Thought alone, his gift concentration, the power of holding a problem continuously in his mind. Keynes placed Newton too at the critical pass of modernity. Newton's spirit looked back to the traditional mysteries of the ancient East—Keynes represented Newton thinking that it was a waste of precious time having to invent the differential calculus when he could instead have been studying the transmutation of matter or the secret meaning of the scriptures. However, Newton was a superb mathematical technician, whose work looked forward to modern science and the West, who translated his insights into the metaphors of scientific understanding (rather than into cryptic signposts towards the transcendental values). Newton '*did* read the riddle of the heavens'.

When George Bernard Shaw wrote a play about Newton, Keynes criticized him because Shaw did not show how *peculiar* Newton was. Newton had said:

I seem to have been only like a boy, playing on the sea-shore, and diverting myself in now and then finding a smoother pebble or a prettier shell than ordinary, whilst the great ocean of truth lay all undiscovered before me. (X:378)

Keynes corrected Shaw, because Shaw had put words in Newton's mouth referring not to the great ocean of truth, but to the 'great ocean of *ignorance*'. Keynes's Newton was a magician who sought truth in the transcendent, while Shaw was presenting him as a mechanist who followed experimental science.

A New Platonism

Although Keynes's distinction between the two causes comes from Locke, he did not accept Locke's empiricism. According to Locke, we draw analogies for our probabilistic deductions on the basis of experience elsewhere, whereas Keynes believed that probable knowledge, which again is knowledge of the world generally, comes not only from experience but also from understanding.

The most important classes of things with which we have direct acquaintance are our own sensations, which we may be said to experience, the ideas of meanings, about which we have thoughts which we may be said to understand, and facts of characteristics or relations of sense-data or meanings, which we may be said to perceive;—experience, understanding, and perception being three forms of direct experience. (VIII:12)

Keynes conceived that the mind has a capacity to see in patterns and to represent its vision in metaphor. Experience tells us nothing, he believed, unless it elaborates an initial insight, and this insight, although it may be mistaken, is not arbitrary but relates to something definite. He seems to have followed Moore; 'It is indifferent to their nature,' Moore had said, in reference to concepts, 'whether anybody think them or not. They are incapable of change' (Moore 1899). But Moore had made concepts, 'whether anybody thinks them or not. They are 'sensible' or a material way. 'Our apprehension of good', said Keynes in reference to his days as a disciple of Moore, 'was exactly the same as our apprehension of green and we purported to handle it with the same logical and analytical technique' (X:438).

In the *Treatise*, Keynes held to the independent reality of concepts, and perhaps he even hinted that they might be innate (VIII:15), but he put good and green on different levels. This is the point of his famous remark that

Moore had a nightmare once in which he could not distinguish propositions from tables. But even when he was awake, he could not distinguish love and beauty and truth from the furniture. They took on the same definition of outlines, the same stable, solid, objective qualities and common sense reality. (X:444)

Keynes distinguished love, truth and beauty from the furniture because he used them to *make* the furniture. The ideas on the other side of the veil are the foundations and support of science and practical judgement. His new idealism was to explain the advance of culture and civilization, in which material and moral

progress must somehow be superimposed on a world in aimless
flux.

In the Preface to the *Treatise*, Keynes said that his philosophy
continued in the English tradition:

It may be perceived that I have been much influenced by W. E.
Johnson, G. E. Moore, and Bertrand Russell, that is to say by
Cambridge, which, with great debts to the writers of Continental
Europe, yet continued in direct succession the English tradition of
Locke and Berkeley and Hume, of Mill and Sidgwick, who, in spite of
their divergences of doctrine, are united in a preference for what is
matter of fact, and have conceived their subject as a branch rather of
science than of the creative imagination, prose writers, hoping to be
understood.

This passage shows how Keynes interpreted English philosophy,
but it is misleading because, as he said later in his essay *My Early
Beliefs*, he did not then recognize the neo-Platonic elements in his
philosophy. 'We should have been very angry at the time with
such a suggestion' (X:438). The essence of Platonism, according
to Benjamin Jowett, former Master of Balliol at Oxford, is that
there is a truth beyond experience, of which the mind 'bears
witness to itself' (Jowett 1953, I:3); and it is also a Platonic
doctrine that only a probable account of knowledge can be given,
since knowledge presupposes classification, and is therefore
inescapably based upon similarity and metaphor. Finally, Greek
philosophy generally began by accepting common experience as
valid, although it had to be interpreted by reference to a higher
model. Each one of those elements is implicit or explicit in
Keynes's *Treatise on Probability*, and none of them is characteristic
of the English tradition of philosophy.

There is a certain paradox, after all, in a philosophy that
begins by declaring that truth is found through prose, which
Keynes did, which pedantically distinguishes between events
and propositions about events, as Keynes did, but which none
the less concludes that all is understood by metaphor in the end.
The English tradition after Locke understood neither fact nor
science in the same way as Keynes. He meant to refute Hume in
Hume's own terms, by pointing out that judgement does in fact
occur on a more or less rational basis, and then offering an
explanation as to how this could be. Although Keynes wished to
confine his argument to prose, his conclusion was that the

foundations of knowledge extend beyond the literal power of words. It is hard to nominate another philosopher in the modern English tradition who makes such a defence of common sense, and whose theories are so opposed to the claims that science is an ultimate system of knowledge. He pursued the theory of organic wholes to its limit; and this theory, Moore acknowledged, came via Hegel. Unlike those philosophers whom he nominates above, Keynes alone argues that science is based upon analogy, and Keynes alone consistently makes intuition and judgement the ultimate guides to both action and knowledge.

To be consistent, Keynes claimed only to give a probable account. 'I do not pretend that I have given any perfectly adequate reason for accepting the theory I have expounded', he wrote in the *Treatise*, although, true to his own theory again, he added that his account of analogy is 'based upon some principle darkly present to our minds'. So he cast himself adrift even from Moore, who had hoped to reach bedrock by being precise in his language, while the influence of Bertrand Russell, who hoped philosophy would progress like science, was purely formal.

Keynes's neo-Platonism conflicts with the widely held opinion that his approach to policy was based on straight common sense. Keynes 'preferred earth to algebra', wrote Professor Klant (1985:90), expressing the usual idea and at the same time neatly reversing one of Keynes's dictums about a statistician who preferred algebra to earth. Nevertheless, I believe that the usual opinion is inadequate because it interprets Keynes by the rules of a philosophy that was not his own. In particular, he did not think that it is necessary to choose between principles and pragmatism: far from it, he believed that pragmatism followed from principle. Uninstructed common sense, or pragmatism without principle, is against the spirit of his philosophy of probability.

Uninstructed common sense seems to be specially unreliable in dealing with what are termed 'remarkable occurrences'. We can only define it as an event which before its occurrence is very improbable on the available evidence. But it will often occur—whenever, in fact, our data leave open the possibility of a large number of alternatives and show no preference for any of them—that every possibility is exceedingly improbable. (VIII:334)

The same point was made later at greater length and less

abstractedly when Keynes drew a character sketch of Bonar Law, a Conservative politician whom Keynes portrayed as having common sense without values or vision:

[Bonar Law] nearly always gave the perfectly sensible reply, on the assumption that the pieces visible on the board constituted the whole premises of the argument, that any attempt to look far ahead was too hypothetical and difficult to be worthwhile, and that one was playing the game in question *in vacuo*, with no ulterior purpose except to make the right move in that particular game. (X:34)

The sketch then proceeded to say that Bonar Law was too shortsighted to avoid future catastrophe, and that his common-sense values led to an inordinate respect for Success. For all his pragmatism, Bonar Law was not successful as a man of action at all.

The usual idea of Keynes the pragmatist is not so much wrong as partial. Harrod put the metaphor more accurately when he said that Keynes meant to create a new earth *and* a new heaven. Keynes took both the high ground and the low, while Hume took the middle. The middle ground is Hume's embryonic philosophy of theoretical science, in which science is protected from values, religion and superstition on the one hand and from casual empiricism on the other. The high ground is Keynes's theory of the intuitive mind, which carries the metaphysical argument for judgement. The low ground is Keynes's commitment to common sense, his inclination (which was encouraged by Moore's philosophy) to accept the 'universal facts of experience', as having almost the status of scientific laws. From Keynes's perspective, Hume was suspended in mid-air, saying both that we cannot trust our ordinary senses and that metaphysics is almost meaningless, only algebra and logic being the routes to knowlege. Keynes believed that the correctness of action is validated by a logic of philosophic discourse, and that, although probabilistic knowledge cannot yield real truths, there can still be a valid basis for what we do partially understand. Whereas Hume had separated truth from experienced reality, Keynes rejoined them by referring to creativity and intuition.

The *Treatise* still forms the beginning point of the modern philosophy of probability, but its anti-empiricist elements have made Keynes's own theories unassimilable among philosophers.

He is now best known for his cogent criticisms of other probability theories, which I have skimmed over here. Keynes is 'dated epistemologically', wrote R. Weatherford in his lucid survey of philosophies of probability (1982:133), adding that few philosophers of the present Anglo-American generation have much sympathy for a system in which 'axioms are part of the *a priori* laws of thought'. Another point is made by R. B. Braithwaite, who wrote the introduction to the *Treatise* in its modern *Collected Writings* edition (VIII: xxi). Braithwaite believed that there could be no such thing as an objective probability if Keynes had to assume arbitrarily the limitations of the human mind; unlike Keynes, he did not conceive of a veil between the mind and the ultimate objects of knowledge.

After the *Treatise*

Keynes's attack upon Hume failed to make headway, but he was not entirely convinced himself, and his ground later shifted. The *Treatise on Probability* and the *General Theory* have a common subject matter, namely the prevalence of uncertainty, and address a common problem, which is whether sensible and rational decisions can be made under conditions of probability and uncertainty. This question had been posed and answered by Hume, who said in effect that they cannot. At first Keynes simply said that, Hume notwithstanding, rational intuitions commonly do occur. This answer defines the *Treatise* as one of Keynes's early works, when Keynes held what he came to regard as his glib belief in human rationality. By comparison, where the *General Theory* later assumed the prevalence of human irrationality, it seemed to turn back towards Hume. In particular, Keynes later said that investors are typically unable genuinely to resolve uncertain situations, and try to follow conventional rules, which is precisely what Hume said about behaviour under probability in general.

Keynes was almost certainly aware that he was conceding a point to Hume when he wrote the *General Theory*. In 1933, a few years before the *General Theory*, he had cited this passage as indicative of Hume:

Tis not, therefore, reason which is the guide of life, but custom. That alone determines the mind, in all instances, to suppose the future conformable to the past. However easy this step may seem, reason would never, to all eternity, be able to make it. (Quoted in XXVIII:388–9)

Although Keynes's *Treatise* might establish the ideal, Hume was right on a point concerning common practice. But if Hume was right to say that people follow conventions, then it is logical that humanity should be subject to the same causal laws as matter, as indeed Hume had thought. If human consciousness were to play a more restricted role, the effect would be to extend objective chance, the dance of the atoms, to human affairs. In the *Treatise on Probability* objective chance is applied to gas molecules and raindrops, but in the *General Theory* the idea is applied to economic action.

As Keynes grew beyond the Platonic Dialogues, with their facile beliefs in the semi-magical properties of the mind, he came to believe that valid intuitions were rare and hard won. But many examples show he always held to the essence of the *Treatise*, which is the *possibility* of a logical probability judgement. For example he wrote, while advocating both peace and the rearmament of Britain in 1936:

The only practicable course is to form a judgment of probability based on our view of the temper of the country, its motives and ideals, its public opinion in the broadest sense, and the sort of people likely to be in power from time to time in the near future. It is on such a judgment, and on such a judgment alone, that we can arrive at a reasonable conclusion whether we wish this country to be strong or to be weak. (XXVIII:52)

Judgement is complex, but following the rules is no substitute. Despite his concession to Hume, Keynes departed further from Hume's philosophy, the middle ground of thought, as logical probability receded.

Keynes's tendency to become more sceptical about the prevalence of reason is the only major variable that needs to be allowed for in this book. Keynes himself located the change around 1914:

I have said that [our] pseudo-rational view of human nature led to a thinness, a superficiality, not only of judgment, but also of feeling. . . .

The attribution of rationality to human nature, instead of enriching it, now seems to me to have impoverished it. . . .
And as the years wore on towards 1914, the thinness and superficiality, as well as the falsity, of our view of man's heart became, as it now seems to me, more obvious. (X:448–9)

It does not follow that the early writings and the *Treatise on Probability*—which was mostly finished in 1914—are on one side of an absolute philosophical divide. To judge from Keynes's economic and political writings, his scepticism continued to deepen; but what changed was the data of his system, while his intellectual framework remained the same.

Notes to Chapter 2

1. Klant was referring to Keynes's criticisms of econometrics.
2. In *The Philosophy of David Hume*, N. Kemp Smith (1966:13) points out that Hume developed his sceptical theory of probability from his sceptical ethics. Keynes drew his theory of probability from his ethics in much the same way; just as judgements of value can be rational even though they are not demonstrable, so judgements of probability can be based on reason. I explain Keynes's probability theory first, because it is (only comparatively) unambiguous, whereas there are widespread misconceptions about his ethics.
3. One principle of which we are aware is the Uniformity of Nature, which says that a change in space and time *alone* does not constitute grounds for supposing that the results of an experiment will change. We cannot learn of the uniformity of nature from experience, and yet neither is it something that must be true, as the principles of logic are. The universe might have been constructed otherwise, but we are aware that it was not. Likewise, we are aware of the principle of causation, that every event has a cause, and (since we don't believe in witchcraft) of the principle that a material event need not have a mental cause.
4. This way of combining the laws of science and the laws of common sense later lead to protest when Keynes referred to the 'fundamental psychological law, upon which we are entitled to depend with great confidence both *a priori* from our knowledge of human nature and from the detailed facts of experience', that an increase in income is partly saved (*GT*:96). Keynes's critics complained that he gave scientific status to what was only a psychological tendency of the time, and so gave his theory an undue generality.
5. These quotes, including the reference to Grote, are all from Cornford (1937:160–72).

3

Rational Ethics

> I am with Moore absolutely and on all things. . . . But as the whole thing depends on intuiting the Universe in a particular way—I see that now—there is no hope of converting the world. . . . It is not a question of argument; all depends upon a particular twist in the mind.
> It is *impossible* to exaggerate the wonder and *originality* of Moore. . . . How amazing to think that we and only we know the rudiments of a true theory of ethic; for nothing can be more certain than that the broad outline is true.
>
> J. M. Keynes to G. L. Strachey, January and February 1906 (quoted in Harrod 1951).

The hallmark of modern thought since its divorce from the metaphysics of the Middle Ages has been faith in the superior logic of science and a conviction that ethics is not rational. The fall of the apple depends upon gravity and not on whether we like the apple. The strongest sign of the division between Keynes and the rest of economics, to say the least of it, is that he believed that there was an ethics subject to the same rules of logic as science, so that ethical and scientific ideas could be intertwined. In the moral science of economics, the fall of the apple depends not only on gravity but also on whether it is a virtuous apple. The boundaries of a moral science stop not where ethics begins, but where reason ends. This is what Keynes implied in his fable of the apple:

I also want to emphasize strongly the point about economics being a moral science. I mentioned before [in the previous letter] that it deals with introspection and with values. . . . It is as though the fall of the apple to the ground depended on the apple's motives, on whether it is worthwhile falling to the ground, and whether the ground wanted the apple to fall, and on the mistaken calculations on the part of the apple as to how far it was from the centre of the earth. (XIV:300)

This account is not entirely unambiguous, as T. W. Hutchison has pointed out, and perhaps all that Keynes meant was that bad apples fall sooner than good ones for the normal scientific reasons.[1] However, there are stronger reasons to suppose that Keynes did indeed believe that there was a true and rational ethics, in which case the implications for his economics and politics are very extensive. Rational ethics would mean a new understanding of economic rationality, and it would mean a rational politics as well. Rational ethics is an obvious link between heaven and earth.

The Connection between Probable and Ought

In 1905, two years after Moore's *Principia Ethica* was first published and in what was virtually a prolegomenon to his own *Treatise on Probability*, Keynes referred in his *Miscellania Ethica* to the 'difficult question of the probable grounds of action and the *curious connection between "probable and ought"'* (my emphasis). Practical ethics would attempt to answer such questions as 'the nature and value of virtue' and 'the theory and methods of politics'. A major theme of the *Treatise on Probability*, and one that has been almost unnoticed, is that, even if there is no connection between what 'is' and what 'ought to be', there is nevertheless a critical connection between what *probably* is and what *probably* ought to be. In the medium of probability, which is the stuff of the world, the connection between facts and values would be re-established.

Keynes found a formal parallel between probabilistic reasoning and ethical reasoning. The parallel had already been drawn by Hume, but for the opposite purpose, namely to deprecate both probable knowledge and ethics. According to Hume, neither probabilistic arguments nor ethical arguments conform to the demonstrable rules of inferential logic, and so both sorts of reasoning are subject to the imagination and are sub-rational. But in practice, Hume's scepticism towards probable knowledge is unworkable, because nearly everything we know is only probable. So the reaction has been to accept Hume's scepticism towards ethics and to forget his scepticism towards probability, which was given mathematical and scientific status. The nineteenth century and, Keynes said, J. S. Mill in particular, had coped with Hume's fundamental criticism of probable knowledge by failing to understand its force. But if non-demonstrable probabilistic knowledge *was* valid, as Keynes believed, then the same reasoning could be extended to and be valid in ethics.

In most branches of academic logic, such as the theory of the syllogism or the geometry of ideal space, all the arguments aim at demonstrative certainty. They claim to be conclusive. But many other arguments are rational and claim some weight without pretending to be certain. In metaphysics, in science, and in conduct, most of the arguments, upon which we habitually base our rational beliefs, are admitted to be inconclusive in a greater or less degree. Thus for a philosophical treatment of these branches of knowledge, the study of probability is required. (VIII:3)

If probable knowledge is valid, then it can only be on the basis of non-demonstrable logic and rational intuition. However, if there is a rational intuition, then it can be equally applicable to ethics. Kant and other philosophers had responded to Hume's scepticism towards ethics by looking for moral imperatives, categorical 'thou shalt' values which should by their inherent nature supposedly be accepted. Keynes believed that Kant had prejudiced the case for a rational ethics by overstating it. By appealing to transcendental 'thou shalt' revelations Kant and other philosophers had forfeited reason, which meant that they were prevented from meeting Hume's hostile arguments on their own ground (VIII:303). By contrast, Keynes tells us that his response might 'conceivably' have satisfied Hume. Keynes's theory of rational ethics does not concern itself with moral imperatives, just as his theory of probability does not try to say what is absolutely true.

The old metaphysics had been greatly hindered by reason of its having always demanded demonstrative certainty. Much of the cogency of Hume's criticism arises out of the assumption of methods of certainty on the part of those systems against which it was directed. . . . The demonstrative method can be laid on one side, and we may attempt to advance the argument by taking account of circumstances which seem to give *some* reason for preferring one alternative to another. (VIII:266)

As we have seen, probability does not lead to truth but only to probability. 'The proposition that a course of action guided by the most probable considerations will generally lead to success, is not certainly true and has nothing to recommend it but its probability.' The rational theory of ethics can be understood in the same way by replacing the 'probability' terms in this quote with 'morality' terms.[2] A course of action guided by the most moral considerations does not lead necessarily to the best result and has nothing to recommend it but its morality. Keynes's rational ethics, in other words, is an ethics of motives rather than consequences. It is similar to the doctrine of Natural Law, the traditional philosophy which advocated the performance of duty, which understood rational action as being correlative with the virtues, the major way in which, the medievals believed, reason could be expressed in an uncertain world.

The modern social sciences virtually begin with the rejection of Natural Law, and Bentham and Hume, whom Keynes regarded as the founders of modern ethics and utilitarianism, both attacked the old system. Rather than duty and the pursuit of virtue being the concomitants of the rational human quest *par excellence*, they held that ethical systems were sub-rational, and that there was no logical relation between what 'is' and what 'ought' to be.

The divine origin and absolute voice of duty gave place to the calculations of utility. In the hands of Locke and Hume these doctrines founded Individualism. The compact presumed rights in the individual; the new ethics, being no more than a scientific study of the consequences of rational self-love, placed the individual at the centre. 'The sole trouble Virtue demands', said Hume, 'is that of just Calculation, and a steady preference of the greater Happiness.' (IX:272)

Kant had begun by endorsing the common morality of duty, but he thought that it had to be ultimately justified by reference to universal moral laws. These failed to convince philosophy generally, and Keynes instead brought in probability—duty was still central, but it had to be intuited according to the circumstances, because pure metaphysics alone can give no rules of action.[3]

The Revolt from Moore

Bentham and Hume won the day, but the issue resurfaced through an unresolved conflict within J. S. Mill, who, although a committed utilitarian, was none the less unable to follow the full utilitarian logic. 'Quantity of pleasure being equal,' Bentham had said, 'push-pin [a parlour game] is as good as poetry.' Mill rebelled against an equation that reduced all values to a single denominator. Yet utilitarianism makes no sense if there are two denominators, one for poetry and another for push-pin, and the virtues, towards which poetry might be a signpost, either stood above utility or they did not.

In the second half of the nineteenth century in England, two philosophies—utilitarianism and intuitionism—vied for supremacy. Utilitarianism was originally so called because it held that desirability of an action depended upon the utility of its *consequences*, whereas intuitionism postulated that the desirability of an act depended upon the quality of the act itself, which quality was understood through the intuition. Intuitionism in important respects continued the medieval Natural Law tradition, although it was a dogmatic doctrine which insisted that intuitions were always correct.

The nineteenth century did not resolve that conflict, at least not if we discount Sidgwick's implausible theory that utilitarianism and intuitionism give the same results; but a synthesis of the two doctrines was one of the main themes of G. E. Moore's *Principia Ethica* (Moore 1929). His philosophy allotted particular spheres to each doctrine. To utilitarianism he allocated the sphere of action; to intuitionism, the sphere of ideals. To this effect, Moore began in the Preface to *Principia Ethica* by differentiating 'what things should exist for their own sakes' from what kinds of actions ought to be performed. He agreed that the good in itself was understood only by intuition, much as beauty was, but he denied that intuition could determine what should be done, so action was in the first instance subject to utilitarian principles. The effect of the division between action and Moore's ideal was largely to take aesthetic sensibilities out of the realm of the utilitarian while theoretically conceding all other behaviour to utilitarianism.

Moore too rejected the Natural Law philosophy. In a chapter of *Principia Ethica* called 'Ethics in Relation to Conduct', he criticized the 'Christian ethics', which said that some things should be done because virtue is won through the performance of duty. Moore said instead that there is no causal connection between ethics and conduct, that duty is outside ethics because it is externally imposed, and that the pursuit of virtue is a narrow end which cannot constitute an aim in life, being even less general than the pursuit of happiness. To convey some of the 'consequentialist' flavour of Moore's argument, and to anticipate a distance that was to appear between the philosophies of Keynes and Moore, Moore rejected the categorical commandment 'thou shalt not lie' on the utilitarian grounds that it was an arbitrary formulation which might or might not lead to good results,[4] whereas Keynes frequently did express a commitment to telling the truth *regardless of the consequences*. To give just one example:

It is such a hopeless business trying to calculate the psychological effects of one's anticipated actions; and I have come to feel that the best thing in the circumstances is to speak the truth as bluntly as one can. (XVII:6)

But although Moore rejected the path of duty on utilitarian grounds, he did not advocate utilitarianism as a guide to conduct, because in practice it was impossible. Moore believed that in practice we cannot calculate the consequences in a complex world in which the reverberations of our actions carry on through endless time. Even in a static sense, if the universe is a complex whole, then it is impossible ever to calculate the effects of our actions, and utilitarianism cannot apply. In addition, the good is so complex that we never know when what we are doing is good.

In order to show that any action is a duty, it is necessary to know both what are the other conditions, which will, conjointly with it, determine its effects; to know exactly what will be the effects of these conditions; and to know all the events which will be in any way affected by our action throughout an infinite future. We must have all this causal knowledge, and further we must know accurately the degree of value both of the action itself and of all these effects; and must be able to determine how, in conjunction with the other things in the Universe, they will affect its value as an organic whole. (Moore 1929:149)

Having eliminated both the motives and the consequences of action as guides to good conduct, Moore advocated following the conventions, for 'we all pretty well know what good conduct is' (1929:3). Provided that everybody else really followed the conventions, and provided that they did not conflict with aesthetic pursuits in the other realm of abstract goodness, Moore felt that conformity to the conventions would be best for civilization.[5] How the conventions can be desirable when there is supposed to be no discoverable relation between ethics and conduct Moore did not say, but our interest lies in Keynes's reaction to Moore's philosophy of action. For although Moore cast this in terms of personal conduct only, the implications are more widespread. If there is no relation between ethics and conduct, then presumably there is no relation between ethics and action generally. Moore meant to advocate conformity with the social conventions, provided they gave free rein to beauty and friendship, but the effect of his philosophy was to deny that any action in politics or economics could have an ethical justification. By implication, Moore denied the possibility of economic and political philosophy and the possibility of statescraft. Later Keynes was to say that Moore was less worldly than St Francis of Assisi, 'who at least made collections for the birds'.

'Now what we got from Moore', Keynes said in his essay 'My Early Beliefs', 'was by no means entirely what he offered us':

He had . . . the other foot in Sidgwick and the Benthamite calculus and the general rules of correct behaviour. . . . We accepted Moore's religion, so to speak, and discarded his morals. Indeed, in our opinion, one of the greatest advantages of his religion was that it made morals unnecessary—meaning by 'religion' one's attitude to oneself and the ultimate and by 'morals' one's attitude towards the outside world and the intermediate'. (X:436)

In the *Treatise on Probability*, Keynes rejected Moore's morals and meant to reconnect what is good with what should be done. He rejected Moore's conventional morals, his 'attitude to the outside world and the intermediate', because he conceived an analytical relationship between action and values in the sphere of probability. This was the precipitating idea behind the *Treatise on Probability*.

It was an important object of Moore's book to distinguish between goodness as an attribute of states of mind and rightness as an attribute of actions. He also has a section on the justification of general rules of conduct. The large part played by considerations of probability in his theory of right conduct was, indeed, an important contributory cause to my spending all the leisure of many years on the study of that subject: I was writing under the joint influence of Moore's *Principia Ethica* and Russell's *Principia Mathematica*. (X:445)

Keynes took issue with Moore's argument that goodness is so complex that no one can ever act consciously for the good; that is, he took issue with Moore's saying that right conduct means to follow the conventions:

Mr Moore's reasoning endeavours to show that there is not even a *probability* by showing that there is not a *certainty* . . . Mr Moore's argument must be derived from the empirical or frequency theory of probability, according to which we must know for certain what will happen *generally* (whatever that may mean) before we can assert a probability. (VIII:342)

To declare that Moore was a Laplacian was strong intellectual language.

Keynes rejected Moore's reason for deviating from utilitarianism, but he also rejected utilitarianism (VIII:344). The outline of this argument is that utilitarianism assumes that the probabilities are quantifiable. (Moore had assumed them to be unknowable and Keynes says neither is the case, that probabilities are a matter for judgement but not quantifiable.) However, by disputing Moore's reasons for deviating from utilitarianism, Keynes was disputing the reasons by which Moore separated values and action.

If the social good is the touchstone for economic and political decisions, then truth, love and beauty are not, which is why Moore had to separate goodness and action. Moore had two deities, the True Ideal in high heaven, and the Social Good as a lesser deity to do any dirty work. When Keynes rejoined ethics and action there was no longer any room for both goods, and his paper on Egoism set out to refute Moore and Christianity by exorcising the Social Good. The argument was that there is no such beast: Keynes would not acknowledge that the Social Good had any mystical existence. 'Why should I not let the universe go to the devil and save my own soul?' he asked. 'It may be that by such action [altruism] I shall increase the general good, that I shall be *doing* good. But *is* the obligation to *do* good? Is it not rather to *be* good?' Much later, in 'My Early Beliefs' (X:437), he disparaged doing good as a social service religion rather than a true one.

Moore, like Hume, had said that practical action is so difficult to evaluate that any attempt to do so must lead to a paralysis of action. Keynes conceded that it *is* difficult to evaluate the best course of action, but he argued nevertheless that it is possible to exercise judgement, or failing that to follow intuitable duty rather than merely to conform to convention. Even if the results of our endeavours are very uncertain (VIII:342), we can still act positively for the good within a restricted ambit, assuming that our good contributes to the whole.[6]

If the *Treatise on Probability* had been understood and accepted, Keynes would have reconstructed what Hume had destroyed, a philosophy of rational ethics. It would not have led to particular conduct, but, in the words of Keynes's *Miscellania Ethica*, it would 'formulate or rather . . . investigate existing general maxims, bearing in mind their strict relativity to particular circumstances'. The most general maxim of a rational ethics involved a return to the primary principle of Natural Law. Rational action for its own sake, as 'a way of life', divorced if necessary from the fruits of action, leads to virtue. We will see that this maxim is the reason for Keynes's various attacks on rational egoism, utilitarianism, Marxism and general 'purposiveness'. It is the moral philosophy that is offered as superior to militarism in the *Economic Consequences of the Peace*; and the same maxim in the *General Theory* elucidates the meaning of rational economic behaviour. Finally, it was to be the moral philosophy of the Keynesian central controllers, and the rationale for the institutional structure through which they would work.

'Keynes-neutral' Economics

In some of his greatest works, Keynes applied his ethics to the most pressing problems of the time, so giving an 'old metaphysics' a fresh and invigorating form. Nothing, he said in *The End of Laissez-Faire*, could be more opposed than the old doctrine and the new: 'the doctrine which looked on the world as the work of the divine watchmaker, and the doctrine which seemed to draw all things out of Chance, Chaos and Old Time' (IX:276).

Keynes also followed the 'modern' doctrine, which took account of chance, chaos and old time; but he meant, by following its logic even more rigorously, to show that some cogs in the old ethical watch were still in place and working. Keynes believed that the economic problem was properly subordinate to 'life and human relations, to creation and religion'. This might not mean much to the modern economist, who normally believes that economic problems can be solved independently of the more fundamental issues to which they are logically subservient; his professional job is to set up a rigorous theory to which any politician can tack on some personal ethics according to his peccadillos. In Keynes's economics, to the contrary, these more fundamental views provide the starting point and not just the goals of economic analysis. Keynes's theory of uncertainty has such an ulterior foundation, and this is why the underpinnings of that theory were misunderstood.

Keynes did not believe that economics should be neutral, in the sense of neutrality that Keynesian economics later came to have, abstracted from freedom and justice. Conventional economists regard economics as rational, but they believe that all values and all political goals are outside rationality. Therefore they believe that professional impartiality requires accepting all goals and values as being on an equal if illogical footing. They make economics the handmaid of politics because they believe that economic intellect should serve the political passions.

'The attempt to fuse together inquiries as to what is, and what ought to be,' wrote Keynes's father, J. N. Keynes, 'is likely to stand in the way of giving clear and unbiased answers to either set of questions' (1904:48).

If political economy regarded from the theoretical standpoint is to make good progress, it is essential that all extrinsic or premature sources of controversy should be eliminated; and we may be sure that the more its principles are discussed independently of ethical and practical considerations, the sooner will the science emerge from the controversial stage. (J. N. Keynes 1904:52)

But his more famous son, who thought that the moral science of economics properly employs introspection and values, did not agree. 'The economist's essential gifts are to be a dealer in the general and the particular, the temporal and the eternal at the same time' (X:174). What is a fact depends upon a system of classification and therefore upon intuition; and Keynes did not think that ethics was as void of rationality as did his father, but rather gave ethics and facts the same status, both being only metaphors for what lies behind the veil. What is more, we will see that Keynes clearly believed that the *material* consequences of an action depended upon its *moral* quality.

The neo-Keynesians correctly see that economic concepts are fundamentally political, and so they regard both economics and politics as ultimately irrational. The main reason for employing economists, according to Joan Robinson in one of her well known and revealing asides, is that the political opposition has them too. Her position also is inconsistent with Keynes, who understood economics ultimately not as a natural science or even as a social science but as a moral science, and who wanted to make both economics and politics more rational.

Keynes believed that a value-free approach was either impossible or uninteresting:

What conclusion do you intend us to draw from your article on 'Complete Impartiality'? Do you want text-books of contemporary political history to be written by persons who have no point of view or *per impossible* conceal it? The object should be, I suggest, that the young should be made aware of the existence of two points of view and of the warmth and quality of feeling attaching to each; and it is unavoidable that warmhearted authors should see some facts through coloured spectacles. (XXVII:43)

Keynesianism strictly implies neutrality, not in the modern sense of being uninterested in justice, or merely declaring one's interests, but in the sense of having as an ideal genuine disinterestedness and justice. People who held to the relativity of all values Keynes accused of being 'uncomfortable in the world' (IX:381), and he wished they would decide for something positive; and we will see that he held that injustice would have, *per se* and regardless of conventional beliefs about values, powerful material consequences. In this fundamental sense, his philosophy is at odds with the philosophy of modern economics and social science.

It is ironical that a Keynesian economic policy is generally thought to be an apolitical or value-free economic policy. The idea comes from a particular paragraph in one of Keynes's most famous essays, 'Economic Possibilities for our Grandchildren', in which he concluded as follows:

Do not let us overestimate the importance of the economic problem, or sacrifice to its supposed necessities other matters of greater and more permanent significance. It should be a matter for specialists—like dentistry. If economists could manage to get themselves thought of as humble, competent people, on a level with dentists, that would be splendid! (IX:332)

Although economists understand this paragraph to mean that economics should be a value-free subject like dentistry, this is not at all what the passage says. If my interpretation of Keynes's ethics is right, the quotation from IX:332 means the opposite to what it is usually supposed to mean. When Keynes concluded that economics should be a matter for specialists, he referred not to value-free economists but to economists who would relate economics to the values that are the matters of greater and more permanent significance. An extensive discussion of ethical purposiveness precedes the quote from IX:332. A purposive person can be put in the nonsensical paradoxical situation where he values not his cat, or even his cat's kittens, but only his cat's kittens' kittens at the very end of catdom. On the other hand, this seemingly irrational psychology is necessary for economic growth; so, while the whole point of economic growth is to develop a different ethical consciousness, for the foreseeable future a false purposive psychology is necessary. The conclusion to be drawn overall is not that economists should divorce their subject from ethics, but that they should clarify their ethics; for it will transpire that this rational ethics, far from being politically neutral, has strong political implications.

Keynes's Vision

To understand the direct influence of Moore upon Keynes's ideas, it is necessary to recognize that Moore's philosophy combined two very different systems. Partly it is reminiscent of utilitarianism; Moore is called an ideal utilitarian, and R. B. Braithwaite has located the 'consequentialist' or practical policy part of Moore in classical utilitarianism. However, this is only part of the story, because the mature Keynes was grateful that Moore had saved him from utilitarianism. The other strand in Moore is associated with his advocacy of the mind-states of beauty, love and truth, plus the related doctrine of composite wholes, which roughly means looking at the entirety of a matter rather than at the sum of its composite parts. Moore also believed that there were 'intrinsic values' or essences underlying tangible things. These doctrines suggest, as Keynes said, 'some sort of relation to neo-Platonism', although Moore squeezed the Platonic concepts into a utilitarian framework.

Moore considered that beauty, love and truth could best be pursued through the 'pleasures of human intercourse and the enjoyment of beautiful objects'. 'Nothing else', he wrote, 'had *nearly* so great a value' (Moore 1929:183). His theory of ethics does not consider that a person who follows his lights might leave art and conversation far behind and enter half willingly into a psychological or literal wilderness. Moore put the ancient ideals, once regarded as the goods of the soul rather than of the senses, into new harness to enhance the enjoyment of a beautiful life. Moore's 'Ideal was a merciful God', Keynes said (X:442). Beauty, love and truth were no longer to be pursued, with only partial success, through a stern virtue, but were to be fully perceived by anyone who had the appropriate aesthetic orientation and the opportunities to exercise it.

Keynes came to reject the aesthetic outlook because it was sterile and narrow. It was also self-defeating: after quoting a typically grey section from *Principia Ethica* on the subject of sensual love, Keynes referred to the 'beauty of the literalness of Moore's mind' which was 'quite free from *fancy*' (X:444). By comparison, Keynes regarded Newton's physics as being very much based on fancy. Yet Keynes still declared that he held to Moore's doctrine of composite wholes, and like Moore he still regarded mind-states as the end of all things. In other words, and as Keynes said, he retained Moore's religion, his idealistic images and his concepts, but he removed the aesthetic construction that Moore gave them.

In his autobiographical essay, Keynes described the evolution of his own thought in terms of a progression from the Platonic *Dialogues* to Plato's *Republic* and then to Plato's *Laws*. Keynes said there that he understood the *Dialogues* to enquire into the meaning of ideals and virtues. It is well known that the *Republic* establishes the nature of the ideal political state which would express and balance the virtues, although at the same time it proves the impossibility of such a pure political state; the *Laws* consider how best in practice to approximate the ideal state by means of law and customs. Overall there is a line drawn, within the Platonic framework, from ideals to political action. Keynes's progression from the *Dialogues* implies that he believed he had effected what Moore and modern economics has assumed to be impossible, which is to bridge the chasm between values and public policy.

Not since the pre-modern period have philosophers accepted the possibility of connecting values and public policy. Aristotle based politics on ethics, but the moderns base politics on the raw facts of political struggle. The argument can be put in terms of Plato's myth about giants who tear up hard lumps of fact and hurl them at the gods, who in turn shoot back thunderbolts of conceptual understanding. When the modern era began the giants declared they had won the battle, and that heaven had disappeared. Moore declared that the battle was a standoff, that the gods still had high heaven although they could not help the earth. Keynes concluded that good ideas and values conquer over material forces, that the gods could win both heaven and earth. (Later he was to qualify this conclusion.)

Keynes believed that he had bridged the chasm with a new ethics which would bear on practical issues, and which, unlike Moore's religion, would apply on earth. At first the new ethics revolved around 'fitness'. A fit object was one which, if the reaction to it was 'appropriate', would lead to a good state of mind. The idea was ambivalent; on the one hand, it meant the priority of aesthetic feelings over conventional morals, the strand from Moore which Robert Skidelsky emphasized in his biography. On the other, it meant the ethics of motives rather than ends, being good rather than doing good, which eventually went into Keynes's economics and politics.

In *Miscellania Ethica*, Keynes split ethics into two branches, one of which was to be a speculative but scientific ethics corresponding to Moore's 'religion'—Moore himself was to be employed to write it for a small fee. The other branch, which Moore was not to write, was practical ethics, revolving around probability and fitness, and concerned with motives and politics.

The second divison—of Practical Ethics—would concern itself with conduct; it would investigate the difficult question of the probable grounds of action. . . . It would also concern itself with the means of producing (a) good feelings and (b) fit objects . . .
  It ought to attempt to answer such questions as the following:
  (i) the nature and value of Virtue
  (ii) the theory and methods of Education
  (iii) the theory and methods of Politics
  (iv) the practical expediency and proper limits of Egoism

(*Miscellania Ethica*)

As this passage indicates, the doctrine of fitness could assign limits to egoism and reconnect ethics and politics under conditions of unquantifiable probability. Keynes argued that organic unities did not apply to aesthetic heaven, but to the real world, to earth, where there *were* close and unpredictable interdependencies between things. Attempts to apply utility theory when organic unities operated led to difficulties—Keynes specifically mentioned the pure theory of economics—whereas Keynes's doctrine of fitness was meant to answer what should be done even if there were organic unities.

We must conclude that from the beginning Keynes understood economics not as a science, but as a method of action. He believed that the utilitarian ethics that had revolutionized economics about 1870 had come to a dead end. Keynes started again, with a new theory of ethics which could apply when the consequences of action are unpredictable and the ultimate goals of human endeavour are hidden but real.

Ideals and the Flux

The new theory still drew on Moore's absolutes. Keynes's advocacy of ruthless truth-telling meant just that, and not some stance in relation to the received pseudo-truths of the day, because he thought that truth was in some sense an absolute. Likewise, when Keynes spoke of justice or wisdom, or against

ignorance and hatred, these terms meant something real and
constant apart from conventional usage. Juxtaposed against this
set of 'intrinsic values' is Keynes's version of the Heraclitean
flux, the axiom that no one can stand twice in the same economic
and political stream. This flux is obviously related to the theory
of uncertainty in the *General Theory*, although it is more pervasive.
The flux, the short run, is the other side of the coin to the
intrinsic values. When Keynes speaks of ideas, their influence is
often said to be in the distant future. By comparison, his short
run refers not only to time but also to this unpredictable process
of change in the world: 'I insist . . . especially on the essential
interconnectedness of the ideas of time and change', he wrote in
an early paper on *Time*. His aphorism that 'in the long run we are
all dead' has been misunderstood, because the utopian author of
'Economic Possibilities for our Grandchildren' did not intend to
declare the irrelevance of the future. Keynes first complained
about the long-run way of thinking in the *Treatise on Probability*,
where he opposed the principle of indifference. By the 'short run'
he meant to emphasize the tempestuousness of economic and
political life, as in this passage from his *Tract on Monetary Reform*:

Now 'in the long run' this [theory that prices are proportional to the
money supply] is probably true. But this *long run* is a misleading guide to
current affairs. *In the long run* we are all dead. Economists set themselves
too easy, too useless a task if in tempestuous seasons they can only tell
us that when the storm is long past the ocean is flat again. (IV:65)

Keynes's vision was partly that all worldly affairs are subject
to change to a possibly large degree, or to what he called
'objective chance'; but it also pointed to an independent sphere
of ideals, appreciable by the mind, by which we might steer
cross-current. It is not a scientific theory but a vision in the real
sense, a metaphysic, or a way of looking at things which may be
suggestive and helpful and true, but which is ultimately
unprovable. It is a perception from a state of mind, arising from
'direct unanalysable intuition'.

I see Keynes's intellectual search and evolution, beginning
with the *Treatise on Probability* and culminating with the *General
Theory*, as an attempt to reconcile the spheres of constancy and
change. Keynes's problem was how to bring truth, beauty and
love down to political and economic earth. To develop a

philosophy of rational values, he analysed terms that were analogous to truth, beauty and love but which took account of the messiness of the real world. Corresponding to truth there was rationality, which took account of uncertainty and moral and probabilistic knowledge; corresponding to beauty Keynes had creativity, the perception of analogy in art, science, business and political judgement; and corresponding to love there was justice, which in practice meant being on the 'extreme left of celestial space'. Each one of Keynes's major three works draws out the implications of one of these three intermediate political virtues. The *Treatise on Probability* is about rationality, the *Economic Consequences of the Peace* analyses justice, and the philosophy in the *General Theory* is organized around animal spirits and the creative impulses.

Apart from these intermediate terms, and underlying them, there was also a direct relation between ethics and the messiness of the world. In the *Economic Consequences* and the *General Theory*, justice and creativity are underwritten by a particular personal virtue. In the *Economic Consequences* the prospect of German revanchism is attributed ultimately to a lack of inner truthfulness on the part of the political leaders of the Allies; and we will see that in the *General Theory* the Great Depression is attributed ultimately to a lack of inner truthfulness in the investing class as a whole. In each instance Keynes described an act of bad faith which was logical from the viewpoint of rational egoism, but which led to an historic disaster, war or depression.

In the early papers this ethic was explicitly applied to personal conduct:

The advantage of truth lies in the greater stability it gives. But it has also a secondary reflex value: suppose true knowledge has not been present throughout the relationship, this will probably diminish the fitness of the story of the relationship regarded as a whole, and hence lessen the value we derive from a contemplation of it. In any relationship there are liable to be two elements of value which are to be distinguished—that derived from the emotion towards him as he is conceived to be at the moment, and that derived from the feeling with which we are filled by a contemplation of the whole course of the relationship. Something which improves the first, a lack of truth for instance, may often make worse the second.

This is an instance of the kind of subtlety with which the subject seems to me to be congested, and which makes the analysis intolerably difficult and obscure. ('A Theory of Beauty')

The advantage of truth lies in the greater stability it gives. An action based on a falsehood can improve someone's prospects from the egoistic and mechanistic viewpoint, but this can often make his overall position worse when the feedback effects are allowed for in an organic unity. However, an analysis of the feedback effects is intolerably difficult and obscure.

Keynes believed that truthfulness is not just an arbitrary value because it is also the prerequisite for intellectual communication. However, we will see that the kernel of Keynes's philosophy, his vision, is that truth is likewise a prerequisite for *correct action*. This is why Keynes was at odds with Hume and the eighteenth-century Enlightenment generally, and why Keynes's philosophy represents a partial return to the medieval and Greek traditions. The difficulty of grasping Keynes arises from the difficulty of grasping the implications of ruthless truth-telling in action. We will now see why Keynes understood those implications to be highly political.

Notes to Chapter 3

1. Hutchison notes that contrasting views emerge from Keynes's declarations that economics is a moral science. 'It is not at all clear just how far Keynes . . . was concerned to "obscure" the "positive" character of economics.' See Hutchison (1981:71).
2. This assumes, with Keynes and Hume, that ethical reasoning has the same structure as probabilistic reasoning.
3. Kant endorsed the common morality of duty: 'The first proposition of morality is that to have moral worth an action must be done from duty. The second proposition is: An action performed from duty does not have its moral worth in the purpose which is to be achieved through it but in the maxim by which it is determined' (Kant 1785:16).

   However, common morality was not defended by reason, and Kant believed that a logical morality had to abstract from the particular circumstances and draw on pure laws. 'We advance by natural stages from a popular philosophy (which goes no further than it can grope by means of examples) to metaphysics (which is not held back by anything empirical)' (p. 29). He was thereby led to postulate universal moral laws, which failed to convince philosophy generally.

4. 'We can secure no title to assert that obedience to such commands as "Thou shalt not lie" or even "Thou shalt do no murder" is *universally* better than the alternatives of lying or murder' (Moore 1929:154).

5. 'Though we may be sure there are cases where the rule should be broken, we can never know which these cases are, and ought therefore never to break it' (Moore 1929:163).

6. The argument at this point is formal and abstruse: if the physical universe is atomic, which is the necessary assumption to justify probability, then goodness too may have atomic elements, meaning that the goodness of the parts may be additive. 'The possibility of knowing that one thing rather than another is our duty depends on the assumption that . . . the goodness of a part is *favourably* relevant to the goodness of the whole' (VIII:342). The argument then proceeds to suggest that the organic quality in goodness does not exclude the atomic or additive idea of goodness.

As Keynes later admitted, there were difficult principles of mensuration in his early philosophy which were not of interest to his later one. On the other hand, the argument raises questions, which I have not addressed, about the extent of Keynes's opposition to consequentialism. Evidently he would not be opposed if life ran according to mechanistic rather than organic rules.

4

The Logic of Politics

To model our principles to our duties and our situation. To be fully persuaded that all virtue which is impracticable is spurious; and rather run the risk of falling into faults in a course which leads us to act with effect and energy, than to loiter out our days without blame and without use.

Edmund Burke (quoted in J. M. Keynes, 'The Political Principles of Edmund Burke')

Modern political theory is based on considerations of power, whereas traditional political philosophy was based as much on ethics. I have said that Keynes's theory of politics was based entirely on ethics. He wrote in the old idealist tradition of political philosophy, which, believing that the state should be ruled by reason and true ideals, was concerned to define the appropriate structure to rule. The tradition also holds, and Keynes himself believed, that democracy and the rights of man can be means but can never have the rank of political ends, because the state has ultimate moral responsibilities, whereas democratic politics are inconstant and are part of the flux. But it had also been traditionally assumed, not as a principle but as a practical reality, that the lot of common humanity was to suffer debilitating and ineradicable poverty. Keynes revised traditional political philosophy in the light of modern economic growth, which he declared to be the most significant change that civilization had ever experienced.

From Morals to Logical Politics

The recognized representative of the idealist tradition in British politics is Edmund Burke, parliamentary orator, contemporary and antagonist of the French Revolution, and said to be Keynes's 'political hero'. Yet it is part of our story that Burke was not typical of idealism because, while property and class had always played a role in idealist political philosophy, Burke enormously emphasized them. In terms of Keynes's metaphor, Burke was on the far right of celestial space, celestial because he based politics on ethics or religion, and on the right because he was committed to the prevailing economic and political inequalities and the constitutional and other feudal conventions that had buttressed them.

Keynes departed from Burke not because Burke based his politics on religion, but because his religion was wrong. Those on the left wing and the right wing of celestial space share a common political philosophy, but they differ as to the facts of its application. Here is an example as to how that difference operates. In 'The End of Laissez-Faire' Keynes drew on Burke, in a very well known passage, to argue that the *laissez-faire* system does not lead automatically to the best result:

We cannot therefore settle on abstract grounds, but must handle on its merits in detail what Burke termed 'one of the finest problems in legislation, namely, to determine what the State ought to take upon itself to direct by the public wisdom, and what it ought to leave, with as little interference as possible, to individual exertion'. (IX:288)

There his quote of Burke ends, but in the original Burke had continued as follows:

Nothing, certainly, can be laid down on that subject which will not admit of exceptions. . . . But the state ought to confine itself to . . . everything that is truly and properly public—to the public peace, to the public safety, to the public order, to the public prosperity. (Quoted in 'The Political Principles of Edmund Burke':19)

As this passage suggests, Burke would be more accurately described as an advocate of law and order than as an economic interventionist. Keynes knew that Burke was opposed to state intervention in the spheres of property or commerce, but he laid aside these circumstantial *applications*, and drew upon Burke's *theory*, which says that ultimately the public wisdom must always be supreme over individual discretion.

Keynes developed his political theories long before his economics, and the principles of his economics reflected his politics rather than the other way around. Nevertheless, the early papers containing his political philosophy remain unpublished in the Cambridge archives. There are five papers there which form a natural group, addressing different aspects of political philosophy with various degrees of overlap. The first written, the longest and the theoretically central paper is a long essay entitled 'The Political Principles of Edmund Burke', and Keynes's politics must be understood in terms of it. Keynes says there that his interpretation of Burke is original. In 'Egoism', he rejects Moore's Universal Good in favour of acting for one's own good, which latter is one of Burke's principles. In 'Modern Civilization', Keynes defines his departure point from Burke and at the same time anticipates his utopian essay, 'Economic Possibilities for Our Grandchildren', written much later. Two other papers, 'Truth' and 'Toleration', can also be regarded as elaborations of 'Burke'. Both Burke and Moore were prepared to forgo truth for practical reasons, and so Keynes defined an attitude to the pursuit of Truth. If however there is a Truth that should be followed, then questions arise about the proper scope for political toleration.

The rest of this section paraphrases the argument in 'Burke', accepting Keynes's interpretation of Burke without question. All references to Burke are drawn not directly from Burke, but via Keynes.

Although Burke is known for his political pragmatism, and is often said to have been devoid of consistent political principles, Keynes began his essay by saying that only Burke had a logical theory of politics. 'Burke is perhaps the only political writer, the direct bearing of whose works is wholly contemporary and topical, who could be approached as the source of a consistent coherent body of political theory'; and Burke did not have any 'appreciable alternation in his general attitude towards the main principles and problems of politics'. The meaning of Burke's pragmatism has been misunderstood—Burke's pragmatism is not inconsistent with, but is an aspect of, his principles. (This is, of course, one of my points about Keynes himself, that the emphasis on his pragmatism has not recognized that this pragmatism is an aspect of a coherent set of political principles.) It is true, Keynes's argument continues, that statements can be drawn from Burke to the effect that 'Nothing universal can be affirmed on any moral or political subject'; but this is consistent with Burke saying that 'Without the guide and light of sound well understood principles, all reasonings in politics, as in everything else, would be only a confounded jumble of particular facts and details without the means of drawing out . . . conclusions'.

Burke was opposed to only one sort of political principle. He did not deny that useful generalizations could be made about politics, but he detested what he referred to as 'metaphysical speculations', or political goals of a universal and supposedly intrinsically desirable nature. Among those metaphysical speculations were liberty, equality and the rights of man generally; but at this point we are considering only the logic of Burke's theory, which Keynes accepted, and not its practical application.

The reason why Keynes believed that only Burke had a logical theory of politics was that Burke based politics on a logical theory of ethics, whereas modern political theory postulates absolute political goals out of thin air. Burke did not accept that there *were* absolute political goals because he thought of politics as a means rather than a set of ends. Burke, says Keynes, 'did not look to establish his ultimate goods by reference to political considerations; these he sought elsewhere'; and 'In Burke's hands the science of politics is concerned with doctrines of means and not of ends. . . . He did not much believe in political ends good intrinsically and in isolation' (p. 81). Burke's ethics entered his politics as concepts rather than as categorical goals, whereas the liberal doctrines that Burke opposed conjured up political goals such as the rights of man and the right to universal representation which were merely arbitrary. Burke complained because, having supposedly disposed of ethics in politics, the liberals had then brought them back in the most shallow way as eternal human rights.

Pragmatism, or the 'supremacy of expediency', as Keynes called it, was Burke's response to materialistic liberalism and the rights of man. Keynes writes of it:

This is not a very recondite doctrine, but to Burke must be given the credit of firstly clearly and insistently enunciating it. It is expedient, he says, that government should have, in theory, sovereign powers, but it must never presume on those powers. . . . We must never confuse 'can' and 'ought'; it is of the nature of government that it should be *able* to do what it *ought* not to do. ('Political Principles of Edmund Burke':37)

It was because Burke formulated this doctrine of expediency that Keynes said that he was 'one of the most extraordinary persons who ever lived', and 'beyond comparison with his contemporaries and in the narrow ranks of the very great' ('Burke':35). Burke rejected political rights, which have no logical foundation, in favour of duties, which follow from deeper ethical principles and the philosophy of action rather than reward.

Dark and inscrutable are the ways by which we come into the world. . . . But out of physical causes unknown to us, perhaps unknowable, arise moral duties, which, as we are perfectly able to comprehend, we are bound indispensably to perform. (Quoted in 'Burke':8)

In politics Burke distinguished between the duty of the government and the power of the government; the power that the government should *have*, which could be limited only by principles of expediency, and the power that the government should *exercise*, which was constrained not by the rights of man, but only by a recognition of the eternal principles of justice and reason. Concerning universal suffrage and democracy, he made a parallel distinction between the power that the people should *have* over government, which again should be constrained only by justice and reason, and the power that the people should *exercise* over the government, which should be severely curtailed, because the people were creatures of prejudice rather than reason. Keynes wrote of Burke's opposition to democratic rights and the formal limitation of government powers:

All these arguments were pressed home by Burke with the utmost power and skill and finally he exposes the root of the whole fallacy: 'By these theorists the right of the people is almost always sophistically confounded with their power.' ('Burke':52)

Burke's argument, which Keynes recognized as valid, was that there can be no rights concerning government, because government is not in the sphere of the transcendental but is only a practical institution concerned with meeting practical human wants. The only right of the people, if it can be so called, is to good government, although the *duty* of the government is to respond to the prejudices of the people wherever possible. Burke opposed equality in favour of both pragmatism and conformity to a higher justice. Keynes called Burke's doctrine political utilitarianism, although he also said that it was unrelated to Bentham, and to ethical utilitarianism.[1] Political utilitarianism meant observing the religious and other prejudices of the people, provided that these were consistent with the principles of eternal justice; it did not mean aiming at pleasures or the desires. It avoided fixed ends of government and recognized the happiness of the people as the only political goal, that is, the goal that is not really a goal, because it is consistent with political duties rather than political rights. The happiness of the people would not necessarily be judged as such by the people themselves.

It was a great discovery—this of Burke's. To clear away the divine right of kings and the French rights of man, to distinguish legal right from moral right, to put an end to the confusion between the power to act and the moral right to use this power, all this is of the utmost importance for all clear and rational thinking on questions of government. It was known before Burke's time that government ought to aim at the happiness of the community; but there were innumerable minor aims and so-called rights that eternally stood in the way. . . . It is by virtue of these 'rights' that tyranny slips in; and where tyranny has been kept out legality in administration has usurped the place of morality. ('Burke':81)

Keynes's pragmatism has been thought to be an aspect of his personality when in fact it was an integral part of his political philosophy. Expediency was conceived by Burke as an alternative to liberalism, but it stands in opposition to all materialistic philosophies; and, as the last sentence of the quote above hints, the principles of expediency were to be used by Keynes as a platform for criticizing both *laissez-faire* and socialism. Like Burke's liberals, Keynes's socialists and free-traders were to see matters of principle in what should have been matters of expediency, and failed thereby to come to grips with the principles of expediency and justice to which they should have addressed themselves.

Although Burkean expediency meant that political policy should be limited only by the most ultimate ethical principles, two important practical maxims, or 'leading rules' as Keynes called them, were almost always to be observed: close attention was to be paid to the feelings and prejudices of the people; and reform must never be violent. These maxims put clothes on the otherwise nebulous notion of expediency, but Burke had derived them from his 'religion' of property and the Church, so Keynes justified them in terms of his own ethics, meaning in terms of either economics or the virtues.

Unlike Burke, the only prejudices of the people that Keynes was prepared to endorse were economic prejudices in favour of work and savings, because, although strictly irrational in themselves, they were useful as a step towards a more rational society. 'We must pretend to everyone that fair [meaning purposelessness] is foul and foul [avarice and usury and precaution] is fair; for foul is useful and fair is not' (IX:331). Other prejudices, concerning religion, property and sex, which were neither fair nor useful, were to be rationalized away and replaced by reason.

Likewise, Keynes did not oppose revolution for Burke's reason, that revolution could destroy those customs and institutions that embody the 'bank and capital of the ages'; Keynes opposed revolution because it threatened literal banks, and literal capital, the modern economic system rather than the traditional moral and political systems.

The economic transition of a society is a thing to be accomplished slowly. . . . The sacrifices and losses of transition will be vastly greater if the pace is forced. This is above all true of a transition towards greater national self-sufficiency and a planned domestic economy. For it is of the nature of economic process to be rooted in time. A rapid transition will involve so much pure destruction of wealth that the new state of affairs will be, at first, far worse than the old, and the grand experiment will be discredited. (XXI:245)

The New Liberalism

I have stressed that Keynes accepted the structure of Burke's political philosophy without accepting the conclusions to which he put it. Burke alone had based his politics on an ethics of means rather than ends, and so only Burke had a logical political philosophy. However, although Burke's ethics conformed to the principles of *reason*, they were not based on *truth*. To say that

Burke had an ethical theory at all is indeed my own misnomer—
Burke believed that the foundation of English politics was
religion, and more precisely the religion of the established
Church of England. 'The majority of the people in England',
wrote Burke, 'consider the Church establishment as essential to
the state, and the foundation of their whole constitution.' By
opting for the Church, Burke opted for the sanctity of property,
the status quo, and in general put peace before truth. Keynes
quoted him thus: 'Perhaps truth may be far better [than peace].
But as we have scarcely ever the same certainty in the one that
we have in the other, I would, unless the truth were evident
indeed, hold fast to peace.'

By 'peace' Burke here means property, the Church, the
aristocracy, limited parliamentary suffrage—all the feudalistic
trappings which, looked into too closely by the superficial mind,
will seem irrational, but which have proved over the centuries to
be the best and wisest form of English government. Compare all
this with Keynes:

> The Church, the aristocracy, the landed interests, the rights of property,
> the glories of empire, the pride of the services, even beer and whiskey,
> will never again be the guiding forces of British politics. (IX:298)

> Mr Burke's principle is that upon which much defence of modern
> popular religion is based. Its truth or falsehood . . . is of the slightest
> importance compared with the . . . support it may offer to conventional
> and convenience morality. ('Truth')

Burke, Moore and Hume all said that convention is the basis
for action, whereas Keynes's vision was that, in economics and
politics, truth is the criterion. Burke did not admit the
'transcendent claim of truth', but argued that in politics truth is
irrelevant or dangerous. The *Treatise on Probability* was a response
to Hume and Moore, to the effect that, even if truth is beyond us,
we can still be rational. However, this was not an adequate
defence against Burke, who recognized the need for rationality in
action but who had a much stronger argument against truth. The
abstract reply to Burke is in Keynes's paper on 'Truth', where
Keynes takes Burke on his own ground and considers whether
there is any social value in pursuing truth. He begins by
admitting that there is none and that the suppression of truth can
usually be justified on some particular ground:

We follow truth because it is truth, and not because we have notified our course by the calculus of probabilities . . . only by an act of faith can we unreservedly and without qualification follow the pursuit of truth, and I believe, at the same time, that this act of faith is right and necessary. ('Truth')

Keynes's politics were not to be based overtly on this act of faith but on a different point. If we do not follow truth we never know whether we should have done so or not:

We cannot establish truth's paramount importance, and yet only by admitting it can we avoid chaos. . . . It is impossible to know what ought to be omitted unless nothing is omitted. We cannot know where to build the walls that are to confine us, until we know where the perils we are to guard against may lie. ('Truth')

Burke had powers of foresight (he prophesied Napoleon, Keynes says), but he was myopic about the new economic possibilities being opened up by technology and capital accumulation. His case for feudalism and property was implicitly based on a continuation of the economic system that had been in existence since time immemorial, in which, by the nature of the economy, the great mass of people were doomed to economic subsistence and weary work. Keynes did not dispute that the feudal inequalities may have been best, given the old economic system, but Burke had failed to see that by preserving the old order he would have choked the new age of economic liberty, in which the civilizing possibilities, which had always been the preserve of the few, could be generally extended. He focused only on the illogical quality of the new political ideas, when he might have recognized that they arose out of injustice, and leavened his political materialism with reason.

'It is a religious war.' It was a war which flung aside all those objects in the mind or in the world which Burke held dearest and most reverent. . . . But if it was a religious war, Burke should have made for it that allowance which all such contests need. . . . He did not ask whether the large ideas, which the revolutionaries set up as their watchwords, might not have an ennobling influence upon men who had lived on the husks of feudalism. . . . He saw that the evangelists of that religion preached their faith with a fervour that did not stop at the exception or regard the qualification. They preached what was not logical. . . . He should have seen in the new evangel the fruitful germs of some of the principles which he himself held dear—liberty and humanity, the moral equality of man, the duties of governments to their subjects, of nations to their neighbours—and hoped that, helpless to eradicate what was fundamental in the old, the new might score broad and deep those lines of morality which earlier systems might have seemed to neglect. ('Burke':75)

With his exceptional powers of analysis and foresight, Burke could have restated the new doctrines of liberalism logically and guided the new age of economic progress with vision. But being too attached to the 'outworks' of civilization, and rendered intellectually rigid by his indifference to metaphysical truth, he saw neither the inevitability of, nor the possibilities in, the new age. Lonely and bitter, Burke was bypassed by events, and the new age came into being on the basis of a political philosophy that could not even be put into coherent logical form.

Keynes's later work, *The End of Laissez-Faire*, extended this picture. There, Keynes said that early liberalism, the illogical political doctrine which initially had good effects, was the parent of both *laissez-faire* and socialism, and that the logical deficiencies of the parent were in its two offspring.

Keynes adopted Burke's logical structure, but he began from truth as well as from Burke's political expediency to create a new doctrine for a new age. In practice, this would lead to the political philosophy of the third way and the formulation of the moral science of economics. I have said in the previous chapter that Keynes began from Moore's religion, which was truth, love and beauty, but that Keynes rejected Moore's morality, which was convention and utilitarianism. It should now be added that he rejected Burke's religion of property and the Church, but adopted his morality, the doctrine of political expediency, which could mediate from the ideals to politics. He combined Moore's religion and Burke's morals, the former saying there are high ideals in heaven and the latter that ideals can be brought down to earth by reason. These ideas contain the germs of Keynes's theories of probability, ethics and expediency, the foundations of the Keynesian system.

In 'Modern Civilization', Keynes took leave of Burke and pointed towards the economic utopia to come. Our duties are no longer to come from convention and the past, but are to be more genuinely based on expediency and the eternal virtues. Keynes did not reject duty, which would be to reject expediency itself, and neither did he postulate some new list of duties, which would have meant conventional religion. Property and the Church would not be duties, and duty would take a more fluid form, based on ideas that could not be tangible. 'All duties are with respect to time and place, and sometimes old duties must go to be replaced by the new.' 'There is and is coming a revolution in duty. We may have reached a critical point in some matters where the general bank and capital of nations [Burke's phrase for conventional duties] and of ages is no longer useful to us.' 'Very little will the primary duties of the future have to do with the . . . fundamental duties of the past.' With the new duties there would be a new philosophy of government: 'Let me quote Burke again; for he expresses the very quintessential opposite of what I wish to maintain.' And he quoted Burke as follows:

We know that *we* have made no discoveries, and we think that no discoveries are to be made, in morality—nor many in the great principles of government, nor in the ideas of liberty. ('Modern Civilization')

Keynes maintained the quintessential opposite to Burke, because Keynes believed that duties could no longer be conventional, that their basis was the ineluctable combined with the circumstantial, and that therefore new ideas of morality with new principles of liberty and government were necessary.

Since the time of Moore we have known that our ultimate goods are eternal and unchanged, sitting at the right hand and at the left hand of God before and behind throughout all time, founded in the nature of things and of goodness, made for man but not by him, the unalterable beacons and rewards of all his efforts. But we have also known that it is not by reference to these alone that our duty is determined. What we ought to do is a matter of circumstance; metaphysically we can give no rules. ('Egoism')

This paragraph neatly summarizes Keynes's philosophy of action. There are higher goods which are to be observed through the pursuit of duty; however, these goods cannot prescribe what duties should be performed without reference to the particular circumstances, and so no general metaphysical rules can be given.

The Garden of Reason

Keynes regarded the modern period as singular, because for the first time in history the economy had made a major secular improvement. Technical progress, which had been arrested since some interregnum between the last two ice ages, was now burgeoning, and capital formation was proceeding on a scale of a hundredfold greater than anything ever previously experienced. Creativity and abstinence from consumption had at last broken the bonds which had always stifled economic growth and restricted access to a higher life to a few. Keynes referred to a 'new order' with new possibilities for prosperity and moral consciousness.

He anticipated that in the fifty to a hundred years after 1930 the economic problem, which had been the permanent problem of the human race, would be solved. The resolution of the economic problem did not mean that everyone would have whatever he might want, because Keynes regarded the economy not as an end in itself, but only as a means towards a state of consciousness. However, it meant that there would be a material surplus adequate for the common pursuit of aims that were inherently superior to the economic, but had always been beyond the range of most people because of poverty and need. Modern life was in a state of transition from one plateau to another, from material frugality to plenty, from conventional morality to the higher life for all.

Yet the transition to the new state was endangered because, while advancing on one front, the moderns had made a critical mistake on another. The mechanistic world view which they mistakenly believed was necessary for the advance of science had led to a false moral philosophy which would jeopardize the anticipated new political order of the world. This is what Keynes meant when he said that Benthamism, meaning also Marxism and materialist ethics generally, was a worm 'gnawing at the insides of modern civilization' (X:445).

Keynes's political programme was to devise institutions that would reconcile prosperity not with utility, but with the pursuit of the good. He believed that sustained prosperity would lead to a higher moral level because the effect of wealth is to deprive purposiveness, or action for the reward, the modern moral error, of its meaning. When the resolution of the economic problem was recognized, rational egoism would eventually be seen as unnecessary, and the pursuit of virtue and of the good would more obviously be the only motive that could be rational.

For purposiveness means that we are more concerned with the remote future results of our actions than with their own quality or their immediate effects on our own environment. . . .

I see us free, therefore, to return to some of the most sure and certain principles of religion and traditional virtue—that avarice is a vice, that the exaction of usury is a misdemeanour, and the love of money is detestable, that those walk most truly in the paths of virtue and sane wisdom who take least thought for the morrow. We shall once more value ends above means and prefer the good to the useful. We shall honour those who can teach us how to pluck the hour and the day virtuously and well, the delightful people who are capable of taking direct enjoyment in things, the lilies of the field who toil not, neither do they spin. (IX:329–30)

Because the modern moral philosophy of purposiveness was widely disseminated after the First World War, the anticipated new order was better foreshadowed by European society prior to the Great War than by postwar society. Before the war economic growth and conventional morality had gone together to create an economic utopia in which there was sufficient material support for any person of character to show his talents, while the working class was reasonably comfortable and content with its lot. Conventional morality meant co-operation and altruism: the working class acquiesced in the highly unequal distribution of income that was necessary for capital formation, while the rich in turn were prepared to forgo the consumption of their high incomes and abstain in the interests of a tomorrow that never seemed to come.

From the egocentric point of view—remembering that Keynes defined modern ethics as the 'scientific study of rational self-love'—the old conventional morality was perverse and irrational, but it had been good in its effect because it led to high economic growth. 'In the unconscious recesses of its being society knew what it was about' (II:12), because the surplus for investment was really very small in comparison to the needs of consumption, and its dissipation by the rich, or appropriation by the poor, would have led to only minor immediate gains at the cost of economic growth in the future. However, the prewar morality which had been destroyed was beyond restoration, and in future economic progress would have to harness rational self-love, which meant consumerism by the wealthy, aggravated class struggle and militarism abroad.

There were therefore two moral forces operating in different directions, both of which were influenced by, and in turn were influencing, economic growth. On the one hand, sustained economic progress could eventually lead to a *rational moral state*, the state that transcends the conventions in the sense that it is consciously moral without being purposive. However, during the transition economic progress would require the motive of rational self-love, meaning that the transition would require a rational amoral state which destroys conventions and is purposive, while its institutions promote the doctrine that morality has no meaning. (The amoral state might have been avoided if it had been possible to pass from conventional morality to conscious morality, but because of the Great War that was no longer possible (II:13.)

The rational moral state is ethically superior to the amoral state—because the aim of the moral state is spiritual goods and a more meaningful good life—and politically superior because only the rational moral state conforms to the rules of justice. For economic reasons, however, the rational moral state can be introduced only gradually, and in the transition the state is in danger of self-destruction because its amoral philosophy of egoism encourages fatal errors of political judgement. The situation is aggravated because the relatively limited supply of creative and intuitive abilities in the amoral state tends to be directed towards science and business rather than towards politics. Although the amoral philosophy may recognize the exercise of rational intuition in entrepreneurship and business, it does not recognize its validity in politics, so that the rational amoral state does not understand the material consequences of its own injustices. There is therefore a critical conflict in the *realm of ideas* between rational morality and rational amorality, between creative and intuitive insights versus the destructive conflicts of egoism, which makes the transition to the new Utopia hazardous.

The remoulding of the world needs the touch of the creative Brahma. But at present Brahma is serving science and business, not politics or government. The extreme danger of the world is, in Clissold's words, lest, 'before the creative Brahma can get to work, Siva, in other words the passionate destructiveness of labour awakening to its now needless limitations and privations, may make Brahma's task impossible.' We all feel this, I think. We know that we need urgently to create a *milieu* in which Brahma can get to work before it is too late. (IX:319)

The moral state that was Keynes's ideal was not the Christian state, or even the 'godly society' as Skidelsky calls it, but the Platonic state, in which reason is a main vehicle towards the good. To draw out the political implications, we may extend one of Keynes's metaphors about prewar Europe (greed and passion played the serpent in the Garden) and say that in the prewar Eden, when morality was conventional, most people did not have a knowledge of good and evil, being unaware that there was a moral choice to be made. After the Great War they went to the tree in the middle of the Garden and swallowed rational egoism, whereupon their eyes were opened and they saw that their previous ideas of conventional morality had been without foundation.

According to the biblical story, the penalty for eating the fruit of the tree of good and evil was to be expelled from the Garden and doomed to live for ever among thistles and thorns. Keynes believed that Eden had at last been glimpsed again after millenia, but he envisaged a return to a better Eden, in which people *could* eat the fruit of all of the trees, including the forbidden one, and enjoy the garden all the more. The dwellers in the Garden would live like gods not only in a material sense; but, knowing the difference between good and evil, they would choose the good. For Platonism, which holds that evil arises only out of ignorance, does not recognize any radical and deliberate evil in human nature.

Herein lies the main political significance of Keynes's recantation, late in life, of his belief in rationality:

We repudiated all versions of the doctrine of original sin, of there being insane and irrational springs of wickedness in most men. . . . As cause and consequence of our general state of mind we completely misunderstood human nature, including our own. The rationality which we

attributed to it led to a superficiality, not only of judgment but of
feeling. . . .
    The attribution of rationality to human nature, instead of enriching
it, now seems to me to have impoverished it. (X:447–8)

When Keynes recanted his belief in rationality, he also recanted
by implication his political utopia, the garden of universal
rational morality, the republic on the left wing of celestial space.
    Newton, said Keynes, was tempted by the devil to believe that
he could reveal all the secrets of God and nature by the pure
power of mind. The author of the *Treatise on Probability* knew
better than to succumb to Newton's temptation, but he was
tempted otherwise, tempted to believe that reason can *guide* all
things. All that was needed to solve a particular problem, he
would say, was a very little clear thinking. In the late 1930s, at
the height and end of Keynes's intellectually creative life, the
fallacy was manifest. Stalinist Russia and Nazi Germany,
'morbid, pathological and diseased' (XXVIII:64) were revealed
to be among the most radically evil powers to have blighted
mankind. The seeds of Keynes's new European order were
choked among thistles and thorns.

The above picture of Keynes's economic utopia has been drawn
from a number of sources, including *The Economic Consequences of
the Peace* and his essays on politics and the future. It is now
apparent that Keynes conceived it much earlier, during the years
when he also conceived his ethical and probabilistic theories,
which means that the economic utopia was one of the first
products of Keynes's vision. The following extract from one of
the early papers shows clearly Keynes's belief that Christianity
would be replaced by a new morality appropriate to the
economic utopia to come.

The old world which took its rise at the dawn of civilization is at last
passing away. There were great transitions at about the time when
Jesus Christ died and was buried, when the medieval world superseded
the Roman, when the medieval world itself gave way. But the greatest
transition of all will be seen, I think, by future rhetoricians and
historians, in the two or three centuries which will have succeeded the
industrial and the French revolutions—a long period of continuous far
reaching ever accelerating change.
    Our [absolute] goods will remain as they must always remain, but

our duties will change. The first and greatest prophet of ends, Plato, will remain the prophet of those who live apart from the machine.

But in the kingdom of moralities and duties the Galilean will himself be conquered, not by words or argument or proof, but equally with his predecessors by the irresistible trend of human affairs and the need for an adequate and relevant morality. He will be superseded rather than destroyed. ('Modern Civilization')

About three decades later, in 'My Early Beliefs', Keynes recanted not only his superficial belief in human rationality but also his criticism of Christianity, by which he meant the conventions.

We used to regard the Christians as the enemy, because they appeared as the representatives of tradition, convention and hocus pocus. In truth it was the Benthamite calculus based on an over-valuation of the economic criterion, which was destroying the quality of the popular Ideal. (X:446)

By the time of the *General Theory* (1936), Keynes had abandoned the republic of his dreams, and his politics shifted from the left wing to the right wing of celestial space, from the future garden of universal virtue to the commercial republic managed by a virtuous élite of central controllers and guided by hallowed customs and laws.

We were not aware that civilization was a thin and precarious crust erected by the personality and the will of a very few, and only maintained by rules and conventions skilfully put across and guilefully preserved. We had no respect for traditional wisdom or the restraints of custom. We lacked reverence. (X:447)

Uncertainty and Fate

Burke was a philosopher of Natural Law. Burke's political thought, says Canavan (1973:665), 'presupposed the doctrine of natural law which had come down through the Anglican tradition from the Middle Ages'. This is to say that Burke believed that there are principles, derivable from human nature as created by God, which apply in the realm of political action. Expediency did not mean ignoring these principles, but it meant applying them to the circumstances, and being not otherwise restricted.[2] In particular, it meant recognizing the element of uncertainty inherent in practical situations and stressing the quality of the motives rather than the ends of action.

One of the new elements in this book is that Keynes's ethics also drew on Natural Law, although he derived it from pure reason and truth rather than the Anglican tradition. He believed, as had Burke, that a violation of Natural Law would trigger a train of events leading to an unpredictable disaster, that there is a 'natural retribution which overtakes evil, working softly in any society' (XXII:75). To abandon Natural Law was to abandon reason itself and become part of the dumb clockwork of the universe, a hostage to fate and the 'hidden currents' which Keynes believed were 'flowing continually beneath the surface of political history' (II:188).

This was the theme of the *Economic Consequences*, which were the consequences following the injustice of the allies to a defeated Germany:

One felt most strongly the impression . . . of events marching on to their fated conclusion uninfluenced and unaffected by the cerebrations of statesmen in council. (II:3)

The automaticity was dramatized by depicting the Versailles Peace Conference after the Great War as a stage on which the principle actors worked out their set roles:

Amid the theatrical trappings of the French saloons of state one could wonder if the extraordinary visages of Wilson and Clemenceau, with their fixed hue and unchanging characterization, were really faces at all and not the tragic-comic masks of some strange drama or puppet-show . . . (II:3)

and in the same spirit again Keynes quoted Thomas Hardy from the *Dynasts*:

Spirit of the Pities
   What prompts the Will to senseless-shaped a doing?
Spirit of the Years
   I have told thee that It works unwittingly,
   As one possessed not judging.

(II:3)

The allies had tried to take what they could from Germany economically and at the same time ensure that she would not again become a military power. Keynes's alternative to this politics of force was a politics of justice, not a modern politics which aimed at the just result, but a Burkean politics[3] which understood justice as a method of action independent of the result.

Even though the results disappoint us, must we not base our actions on better expectations, and believe that the prosperity and happiness of one country promotes that of others, that the solidarity of man is not a fiction, and that nations can still afford to treat other nations as fellow creatures. (II:170)

Keynes believed that the effect of retribution was to thwart what was most desired in the first place. For example, German militarism was responsible for the bull-headed military tactics that cost Germany the First World War; and later the French attempts to win security by destroying Germany created a military nemesis for France.

The inevitable workings of its own essence [German militarism] brought down upon itself the great defeat. (X:52)

Each guarantee that was taken, by increasing irritation and thus the probability of a subsequent *revanche* by Germany, made necessary yet further provisions to crush. (II:22)

If we aim deliberately at the impoverishment of Central Europe, vengeance, I dare predict, will not limp . . . before which the horrors of the late German war will fade into nothing. (II:170)

Likewise, the venality and greed of the victorious powers led to the ruination of their own economies, because they failed to understand what German reparations meant for their own industries, or to recognize the fragile and interrelated nature of the European economies. The victorious powers 'gave way to passion and greed, and became blinded to the real facts of the economic structure of Europe, and even to their own self-interest' (II:xxv).

Purposive morality was not only irrational, but inexpedient, because it involved a self-deception, and to stop short of the truth is to become unaware of the point at which it becomes necessary. All of the allied negotiators at Versailles had based their positions on some deep refusal to accept relevant facts. 'It was necessary to ignore the facts entirely. The resulting unveracity was fundamental', Keynes wrote of the Italian and French positions (II:94); and he made similar observations about the British and Americans. The negotiators at Versailles turned from truth towards some seemingly advantageous self-deception which eventually became self-defeating because the chain of consequences was not thought through.

Now, if Burkean Natural Law applies in politics, why should it not likewise apply in economics? If there is a violation of rational morality in economics, would there not likewise be a retribution in kind?

Notes to Chapter 4

1. Skidelsky, who regards Keynes as a utilitarian, assumes that Keynes understood Burke in the same light. See for example Skidelsky (1983:154–7). Keynes's description of Burke as a 'political utilitarian' is highly misleading, because analysis of the text shows that so-called political utilitarianism was understood by Keynes to be an ultimately religious, rather than secular, doctrine. The essay began with Keynes complaining of the 'unqualified and undue stress laid on his [Burke's] detestation of general principles', and 'Mr Morley, in particular, has been led away by his utilitarian sympathies to underrate the extent of Burke's belief in intrinsic and universal goods.' Keynes then proceeded to argue that Burke was not an ethical utilitarian but thought in terms of good and evil, and referred to Burke's 'original ideas of rectitude, to which the mind is compelled to assent when they are proposed'. Finally, he referred to Burke's commitment to duty, and quoted Burke's belief that the desires of the people are only to be followed 'when they do not militate with the stable and eternal rules of justice and reason'. See 'The Political Philosophy of Edmund Burke':1–9.

   Burke was a political utilitarian because he followed the doctrine of expediency, instead of being dogmatically bound to the liberal ideology which was then gaining ground. He promoted the happiness of the people, which happiness came from convention and religion, and certainly not from individual choice. Keynes's account of Burke is remarkable because at the time that Keynes wrote his essay, Burke was generally regarded as a utilitarian. However, Keynes anticipated the scholarship that radically changed the picture more than half a century later.

2. 'By Natural Law Burke always meant essentially the same thing, and he applied it as the ultimate test of justice and liberty in all human

affairs. As a practical statesman he feared abstractions and was reluctant to take his mind from concrete political problems. But to Burke no *moral* problem was even an *abstract* question; he therefore conceived of statecraft as the practical application in concrete human affairs of primary moral principles, clearly evident to man's right reason' (Stanlis 1958:95).

3. 'Burke conceived conquest in time of war as an act securing not merely physical power over an enemy, but also dictating a profound moral responsibility upon the victorious state, compelling it, under threat of forfeiting its acquired sovereignty, to grant the defeated people *"an equitable government"* based on Natural Law' (Stanlis 1958:93).

PART II

Economics

5

The Meaning of Uncertainty

I returned, and saw under the sun, that the race is not to the
swift, nor the battle to the strong, neither yet bread to the
wise, nor yet riches to men of understanding, nor yet favour
to men of skill; but time and chance happeneth to them all.

Ecclesiastes

Although Keynesian economics is called the economics of
uncertainty, the meaning of uncertainty raises problems. The
General Theory seems to contradict the *Treatise on Probability*; the
Treatise was about actions on the basis of imperfect knowledge,
but when we pass to the *General Theory* even partial knowledge
of the future seems to be assumed away. The wide definition of
probability in the *Treatise* is replaced by a radical definition of
uncertainty which gives no scope for the rational intuitions of the
mind. Not only the variables of knowledge, but also the
parameters within which thought occurs, are liable to unpredictable major shifts. The twilight of probability turns to dark night.

Even the weather is only moderately uncertain. The sense in which I am
using the term is that in which the prospect of a European war is
uncertain, or the price of copper and the rate of interest twenty years
hence, or the obsolescence of a new invention, or the position of private
wealth-owners in the social system in 1970. About these matters there is
no scientific basis on which to form any calculable probability whatever.
We simply do not know. (XIV:113)

Yet despite this apparent nihilism, I will show that the theory
of uncertainty was not a refutation of Keynes's earlier vision but
a continuation and elaboration of it, amended to allow for
irrational behaviour. Keynes's theory of uncertainty, like his
theory of probability, has to be understood from an idealist
perspective, but this time in terms of a departure from rational

ethics. The theory of uncertainty is an instance of Keynes's dualism between the actual and the ideal.

When he was writing the *General Theory* Keynes put the argument in Marxian terms. He distinguished an entrepreneurial economy from a co-operative economy, which latter had money but did not think in capitalistic ways. What mattered was not money in itself, but the prevailing attitudes to it, the psychology of business. This distinction, Keynes acknowledged, bore 'some relation' to the one made by Marx (XXIX:81).

A fundamental law of classical economics is Say's Law, which says that there cannot be involuntary unemployment because total demand in the economy must equal total supply, since all incomes are spent in one way or another. However, if money is hoarded, then total demand *will* fall short of total supply. Say's Law assumes that no money will be hoarded, and so all theories of involuntary unemployment must explain why there should be hoarding. Marx had used the distinction between a capitalist economy and a pre-capitalist co-operative economy to explain why hoarding of money did in fact occur.

In a co-operative economy, the Marxian theory runs, the psychology of exchange is C–M–C', where commodities (C) are turned into money (M) for the purpose of obtaining other commodities (C'). Under these conditions, there is no hoarding of money because there is no reason to hoard. However, under capitalist conditions the psychology of business is M–C–M', meaning that business parts with money in order to obtain more money. Accordingly, there can be a reason to hoard money, Say's Law fails, and there can be unemployment.

Keynes acknowledged that the Marxian distinction between the two processes of exchange was revealing, although he said that Marx had gone on further to error. The Marxian theory is that there is a long-run tendency for M' to exceed M as surplus value is manifested. Keynes believed that the difference between M and M' was a monetary phenomenon rather than a long-run phenomenon, and so he thought that Marx was wrong to say, other than in inflationary periods, that M' exceeds M.

The excess of M' over M is the source of Marx's *surplus value*. It is a curiosity in the history of economic theory that the heretics of the past hundred years who have, in one shape or another, opposed the formula M–C–M' to the classical formula C–M–C', have tended to believe *either* that M' must always and necessarily exceed M or that M must always and necessarily exceed M', according as they were living in a period in which the one or the other predominated in actual experience. Marx and those who believe in the necessarily exploitatory character of the capitalist system, assert the inevitable excess of M'; whilst Hobson, or Foster and Catchings, or Major Douglas, who believe in its inherent tendency towards deflation and under-employment, assert the inevitable excess of M. (XXIX:82)

Keynes accepted the essential point that C–M–C', the co-operative psychology of limited gain, meant economic stability; whereas M–C–M', the entrepreneurial psychology of unlimited financial gain, led to economic instability. He also believed, as did Marx, that the C–M–C' psychology had become very difficult to exercise under modern economic conditions. He understood unemployment in terms of a departure of actual behaviour from the norm of a co-operative economy. The entrepreneurial or M–C–M' economy departed from the rules of a co-operative or C–M–C' economy, which departure led to hoarding, fluctuations in demand and unemployment:

There is a difference of the most fundamental importance between a co-operative economy and the type of entrepreneur economy in which we actually live. For in an entrepreneur economy, as we shall see, the volume of employment, the marginal disutility of which is equal to the utility of its marginal product, may be 'unprofitable' in terms of money. The explanation of how output which would be produced in a co-operative economy may be 'unprofitable' in an entrepreneur economy, is to be found in what we may call, for short, *the fluctuations of effective demand*. (XXIX:79–80)

Fluctuations therefore do not occur in the C–M–C' economy, but economists had looked for regularities in the M–C–M' relation without reference to the criterion of C–M–C', whereas in fact M–C–M' is only an inconstant surface relation.

Marx, however, was approaching the intermediate truth when he added that the continous excess of M' would be inevitably interrupted by a series of crises, gradually increasing in intensity, or entrepreneur bankruptcy and underemployment, during which, presumably, M must be in excess. My own argument, if it is accepted, should at least serve to effect a reconciliation between the followers of Marx and those of Major Douglas, leaving the classical economists still high and dry in the belief that M and M' are always equal! (XXIX:82)

Keynes believed that he stood intermediate between Marx and the monetary heretics, not because he believed that M was equal to M′, which was the classical theory, but because he did not believe that there were regularities in the prevailing M–C–M′ system. However, Keynes did see regularities in the co-operative or C–M–C′ economy, and the aim of economic policy was to bring M–C–M′ into conjunction with C–M–C′. Now the M–C–M′ psychology of unlimited gain suggests maximization, while C–M–C′ corresponds to the unpurposive morality.[1]

Irrationality and Instability

In the *General Theory* Keynes identified uncertainty as the pivot of the actual economic system. Expectations of the future determine investment, which in turn determines aggregate demand and employment through a spending multiplier. The economy is volatile because expectations and investment are volatile. However, uncertainty was not a vague background context, but was at the heart of a moral as well as a probabilistic philosophy which implied a different way of understanding the economy. The major fault of the classical theory of economics was that it had failed to understand the implications of uncertainty. The reason why investment is unstable is that the reaction of the average investor to uncertainty is radically irrational, in a way that economics had not recognized as meaningful. Uncertainty refutes Benthamism and shows that the psychology of unlimited gain is irrational:

The orthodox theory assumes that we have a knowledge of the future of a kind quite different from that which we actually possess. This false rationalization follows the lines of the Benthamite calculus. The hypothesis of a calculable future leads to a wrong interpretation of the principles of behaviour which the need for action compels us to adopt, and to an underestimation of the concealed factors of utter doubt, precariousness, hope and fear. (XIV:122)

In neo-classical economic doctrine each person is assumed to be rational, meaning that he makes the most effective use of his time and money, given the market information and given his inclinations and the state of his mind. He is assumed to maximize his satisfactions or utility, to choose more rather than less in a consistent way. However, rational economic man is not rational in Keynes's sense, partly because rational economic man overlooks that a set of satisfactions accepted also confirms within himself a set of concealed concepts and values.

They lack altogether the kind of motive, the possession of which, if they had it, could be expressed by saying that they had a creed. They have no creed . . . whatever. That is why . . . they fall back on the grand substitute motive . . . money. . . . [They] flutter about the world seeking something to which they can attach their abundant *libido*. But they have not found it. They would so like to be apostles. But they cannot. They remain business men. (Abridged from 'Clissold', IX:320)

Rational economic man, as a utilitarian, also overlooks the probabilistic basis of factual knowledge. Utilitarianism assumes that people are maximizing their position, when in fact most economic decisions are made under conditions of probability with chances that cannot be quantified. When there is uncertainty, maximization does not make sense, because there is no meaningful way of knowing the quantitative odds except by inventing them artificially. Yet since decisions *are* being made all of the time by rational economic men who believe that they *are* maximizers, another way of thinking was being adopted beneath the surface. 'How do we manage in such circumstances', he asked after the *General Theory*, 'to behave in a manner which saves our faces as rational, economic men?' (XIV:114).

Keynes' answer in the *General Theory* was that people tend to adopt various *conventions*, which represent the economic and political parameters as more stable than they actually are. 'We have tacitly agreed, as a rule,' said Keynes, 'to fall back upon a convention . . . that the existing state of affairs will continue indefinitely, except in so far as we have reason to expect a change'; and 'the psychology of a society of individuals, each of whom is endeavouring to copy the others, leads to what we may strictly term a *conventional* judgment.' Within the framework of the convention it is possible to make a 'good Benthamite calculation of prospective advantages and disadvantages' of investment. Yet, however valuable these conventions might be, and Keynes said they were compatible with a considerable measure of continuity and stability of affairs, they were inferior to the prudence that could take direct cognizance of the powers and uncertainties of the world. The convention can preserve stability only so long as it is reliable. 'It is not surprising that a convention, in an absolute view of things so arbitrary, should have its weak points. It is its precariousness which creates no small part of our contemporary problem of securing sufficient investment' (*GT*:153).

I do not agree therefore with the Keynesian socialists when they say that Keynes de-emphasized profit-maximizing and turned economics into the study of business conventions.[2] Keynes did not differentiate, but rather bracketed together, profit-maximizing and following the economic conventions. When investors try to follow a profit-maximizing strategy they cannot really do so, because of uncertainty. They can *act* as though they are maximizing profits if they assume certain conventions, such as that economic conditions will be the same in the future as today. But this is irrational behaviour in terms of Keynes's ethical theory.

In Keynes's theory, the conventions fall short because they only rationalize the underlying motives for investment. The tendency to discount contingency outside the convention subtly preserves values that are partly based upon a self-deception. The question that Keynes's analysis asks, and which its interpreters have not entertained, is whether this widespread self-deception affects the qualitative nature of the economy. Keynes's answer in paraphrase was that a gravitational tendency towards bad faith is ultimately responsible for the instability of the capitalist system.

It is the psychology of utter irrationality that causes the volatility of investment behaviour. In his explanation of the *General Theory* in the *Quarterly Journal of Economics*, Keynes wrote:

[Action] based on so flimsy a foundation, it is liable to sudden and violent changes. . . . New fears and hopes will, without warning, take charge of human conduct. The forces of disillusion may suddenly impose a new conventional basis of valuation. . . . At all times the vague panic fears and equally vague and unreasoned hopes are not really lulled, and lie but a little way below the surface. (XIV:115)

Keynes frequently emphasizes and reiterates that investors do not know the future consequences of what they do today. The significance of uncertainty in Keynes's analysis is that it disconnects the reward of action from its motive. The investor is obliged to choose, but he is apparently without a basis for choice, so that 'without a definite and calculable future' any rational reaction *in the sense of economic man* is impossible. In the *General Theory* Keynes partly conceded to Hume's theory that all action is irrational or based on self-deception: when the average investor is faced with uncertainty, he resorts to insincerity to himself, using evasions to deny that the uncertainty really exists, in order to reach a decision.

Evasion deprives the speculators of a genuine volitional choice of action. It would be rash, Keynes said, to predict the reactions of the average businessman, but they are moved by the social and political atmosphere and by their own 'hysteria and digestion and reactions to the weather'. Theirs is causation without regularity, determinateness without any pattern that could be described by antecedents or scientific laws. It is the herd of mass opinion feeding upon itself, in which the more clever members of the group are only the more voracious.

We have seen how Keynes traced the origins of utilitarianism to Hume: 'Reason is and ought to be the slave of the passions, and can never pretend to any other office than to serve and obey them'; and Keynes said that Bentham had only extended Hume's maxim from the personal to the social sphere. The neoclassical economists in turn had followed Bentham, but Keynes said that Bentham forgot the 'cynical' corollary in Hume's philosophy, that action and reason are irreconcilable (IX:274). Hume had said reason is the slave of the passions partly because the mind cannot deal with uncertainty, but the economists had adopted Hume's maxim and then left uncertainty out of their theories; they adopted the utilitarian maxim but forgot its premise. Consequently, uncertainty recognized confronts rational economic man with the insoluble Humian puzzle, what we do when we do not know the consequences of what we do? In the frame of rational economic man, the problem has no answer.

Keynes makes a moral *quality* of behaviour determine the *facts* of behaviour. The problem is not, as G. L. S. Shackle has said, that rational behaviour is meaningless for the investor, but that rational behaviour has no meaning *within the utilitarian framework*. Keynes did not believe that rationality, the C–M–C' psychology, was at fault, but the opposite, that utilitarianism, or the

M–C–M' psychology, was at fault. His criticisms of utilitarianism are extensive; nowhere does he say that reason is impossible. He was not trying to contract the proper sphere of reason, but to show that a particular failure of (moral and probabilistic) reason had wider effects than had been understood.

Rationality under Uncertainty

In the *General Theory* Keynes considered a capitalist economy that would be genuinely self-regulating. Referring to an age which he described only as being 'in former times', he said that investment was not conducted ultimately for profit, because no one really knew what the profit rate was, either in the future or on the average. Business was conducted instead as a way of life, and an avenue for action and creation.

In former times, when enterprises were mainly owned by those who undertook them or by their friends and associates, investment depended on a sufficient supply of individuals of sanguine temperament and constructive impulses who embarked on business as a way of life, not really relying on a precise calculation of prospective profit. (*GT*:150)

In that golden age, macroeconomic intervention by the government to stabilize the economy was unnecessary. But now that age is past; 'Thus if the animal spirits are dimmed and the spontaneous optimism falters, leaving us to depend on nothing but a mathematical expectation, enterprise will fade and die;—though fears of loss may have a basis no more reasonable than hopes of profit had before' (*GT*:162).

It would be wrong to force a utilitarian interpretation upon these passages, and they do not mean that investors would obtain more utility from present instead of future gratification. They mean that entrepreneurs can act rationally under uncertainty only if they accept the action for its own sake and not for its fruits. Keynes's solution to Hume's paradox in the *General Theory*, as in the *Treatise on Probability*, is that if judgement is dubious or impossible a rational response to an unpredictable future requires a commitment to the act but a dispassion to the consequences; uncertainty requires the emphasis to be put on the motives rather than the end. Putting it in another way, it means recognizing the organic context and not merely the immediate repercussions of action. This is what rational ethics means in Keynes's terms, and what animal spirits mean in the *General Theory*.

Most, probably, of our decisions to do something positive, the full consequences of which will be drawn out over many days to come, can only be taken as a result of animal spirits—of a spontaneous urge to action rather than inaction, and not as the outcome of a weighted average of quantitative benefits multiplied by quantitative probabilities. (*GT*:161)

The phrase 'animal spirits' first appears in Plato's *Republic* (375e); they were so called because action without reward reminded Plato of a dog, which does not distinguish between who feeds him or not, but only does his duty. Dr A. Dow and Dr S. Dow speculated that Keynes had drawn on some original 'Babylonian' meaning of animal spirits,[3] and evidently he has used the phrase in something like its literal sense.

The *General Theory* expressed the same ethics that Keynes had developed in the *Treatise on Probability*, and which was also the same ethics underlying Burkian politics. In economics it was animal spirits, in politics it was expediency and duty, in philosophy it was fitness, in political economy it was purposelessness, and generally it was intuitive judgement supplemented by the logic of means rather than ends. Although Keynes conceded to Hume that most people are irrational, none the less, the Platonic *criterion* of rational action was unchanged.

In the *Treatise on Probability*, Keynes once expressed the criterion in this way:

Herodotus puts the point quite plainly. 'There is nothing more profitable for a man', he says, 'than to take good counsel with himself; for even if the event turns out contrary to one's hope, still one's decision was right, even though fortune has made it of no effect: whereas if a man acts contrary to good counsel, although by luck he gets what he had no right to expect, his decision was not any the less foolish.' (VIII:339–40)

When the investors lose their animal spirits they become subjective and irrational and the economy becomes volatile. They act contrary to good counsel, hoping by luck to get what they have no right to expect, although their decisions are no less foolish even if their luck holds. Keynes's theory of uncertainty has a subjective element, which concerns common behaviour, and an objective element, which is the rational criterion.

In his ethical writings, Keynes put the point in a different way again. 'We can often—if we know enough—say what, apart from peculiar circumstances, a man *ought* to think and feel. Not indeed what he *can* think and feel—that will depend on his nature and his past' ('A Theory of Beauty').

We can say in a general way what the capitalist *ought* to do, which is to follow his animal spirits. But we cannot say what he *will* do, which, depending as it does on his nature and his past, contains an arbitrary element. Action is aberrant, but there is an objective ideal.

Radical Irrationality

Keynes was not the only economist to have an objective theory of action. 'Judgment has in an effective sense a true or objective value', wrote the American economist Frank Knight. There is a remarkable parallel between the theories of Keynes and Knight which is based upon, but goes beyond, the logical theory of probability. The nature of this parallel has been overlooked, because Knight disavowed any interest in the philosophical setting of his theories and presented them simply as the economics of entrepreneurship, whereas Keynes made a frontal attack on the prevailing philosophic orthodoxy. Consequently, while the modern philosophy of probability arose largely in opposition to Keynes's *Treatise on Probability*, Knight's work has been both widely praised and largely ignored.

Like Keynes, Knight drew on the principle of indifference (although he does not call it that) to criticize Laplacian statistical methods—'the entire science of probability in the mathematical sense is based on the dogmatic assumption that the alternatives are really equally probable'—and like Keynes, he differentiated between quantitative risk and the more realistic case in which there is some information about the future but not enough for a strict deduction.

Like Keynes again, Knight drew upon Locke to differentiate between the two meanings of causation, which he related to the 'substratum' (*causa essendi*) and the 'attributes' (*causa cognoscendi*) of things. He pointed out that most of what we know is at the level of the attributes, so that for the most part our knowledge is only analogical. 'We must use the principle that things similar in some respects will behave similarly in certain other respects even when they are very different in still other respects.' However, he believed that we have a faculty of judgement and a partial power to anticipate the future, based upon our capacity to classify, which capacity Knight (unlike Keynes in this respect) regarded as being no more than an extension of the ordinary powers of sensation and perception. He also elaborated at length on a point subsequently made by Keynes, that there are evolutionary reasons to expect such a capacity to develop.

Knight recognized such a faculty would be highly fallible, and he too drew up a picture of action in an elusive and indeterminate world:

A law of change means given behaviour *under given conditions*. But the 'given conditions' of the behaviour of any object are the momentary states and changes of other objects. Hence the dogma of science, that the world is 'really' made up of units which not only do not change. . . . We have examined this dogma and been forced to the conclusion that, whatever we find it pleasant to assume for philosophic purposes, the logic of our conduct assumes real indeterminateness, real change, discontinuity. (Knight 1921:314)

Yet Knight's economics of uncertainty is markedly less radical than the economics of uncertainty in the *General Theory*. Knight said (1921:18) that the purpose of his book was to bring out the assumptions underlying 'natural price' theory, and although he said that perfect competition was not possible, he still assumed that the (Ricardian) system of natural prices was the economic norm, even if an imperfect one. He did not conceive that the economic system might break down because of uncertainty, and the emphasis in his book was on the various ways in which uncertainty could be lessened; uncertainty modified the abstract scientific picture without really threatening its validity. For example, he said of the classical theory of interest that 'it is quite unnecessary to believe that there will really be any progress towards equilibrium, and it goes without saying that the failure of such progress to occur militates against neither the logical soundness nor the practical utility of the theory itself' (p. 168).

Knight believed that the consolidation of firms in the economy would help to overcome uncertainty, and that, theoretically, consolidation would reduce uncertainty altogether. The degree of consolidation was limited by a 'moral hazard', which arose because agents, meaning salaried executives, would be better able to pursue their own narrow interests as this consolidation proceeded. Therefore the validity of the competitive natural price theory depended upon the truthfulness of the agents and executives chosen by the entrepreneur, whose highest task was to make such a judgement of character. 'In a world where uncertainty plays so great a part as it does in our progressive private-property society, the virtue of truthfulness becomes the very pearl of character.' In short, Knight believed, and later declared very explicitly, that economics is a moral science that interweaves judgements of fact and real values. Knight also subscribed to Keynes's idea that there is a relation between ethics and probability, and that rational action constitutes a process rather than an end. 'The real motive', he said, 'is the desire to excel' (Knight 1921:360).

Knight regarded the Ricardian science of economics as compatible with the moral science of economics because he believed that economic behaviour is *typically* creative and rational in a higher sense. Whereas Keynes thought that 'rational morality' was no longer easy in a modern economy, Knight believed that it was still the norm, and that business was conducted not for profit but for the purpose of creation; Knight still believed in animal spirits.

The business man has the same fundamental psychology as the artist, inventor or statesman. He has set himself a certain work and the work absorbs and becomes himself. It is the expression of his personality; he lives in its growth and perfection according to his plans. (Knight 1921:163)

He believed that uncertainty could be conquered by the creative business flair of the entrepreneur, who takes 'more interest in action whose fruition is only probable than he would if it were certain'. In this and other ways Knight drew up a picture of the 'former times' which Keynes mentioned in the *General Theory*, the C–M–C' psychology which Knight regarded as still a true picture of capitalism.

This was the opposite to Keynes, who said that enterprise had become a bubble on a whirlpool of speculation, and investment a byproduct of the activities of a casino. Speculation was the activity of forecasting the psychology of the market, and under modern conditions it would necessarily overshadow enterprise:

Investment based on genuine long-term expectation is so difficult today as to be scarcely practicable. He who attempts it must surely lead much more laborious days and run greater risks than he who tries to guess better than the crowd how the crowd will behave; and, given equal intelligence, he may make more disastrous mistakes. . . . It is the long-term investor, he who most promotes the public interest, who will in practice come in for most criticism, wherever investment funds are managed by committees or boards or banks. For it is in the essence of his behaviour that he should be eccentric, unconventional and rash in the eyes of average opinion. (*GT*:157)

Knight did not mention such irrational uncertainty, and his account of capitalism made bare reference to the hopes and fears and other phantoms of the mind which become the centre of economic gravity in the *General Theory*. 'Uncertainty' in Knight's *Risk, Uncertainty and Profit* means virtually the same as 'probability' in Keynes's *Treatise on Probability*. It is not quantitative; it is subjective, but it *is* rational and as a result uncertainty is contained.[4]

The meaning that Keynes gave to uncertainty in the *General Theory* has no analogue in Knight. Because he believed that creative rationality was the dominant investment psychology, Knight could accept the river of change in an abstract sense, and yet not apply it systematically to the economy. Whereas Keynes had come to regard the virtue of truthfulness and the associated powers of analogical reasoning as abnormal, Knight still regarded the problem of marshalling them as technical. It is arguable that the difference one stage back is that Keynes thought that creativity had a transcendental source, and that Knight did not. In any event, what this comparison of Keynes and Knight shows is the extent to which the *General Theory* depends upon Keynes's scepticism towards rationality, and the significance of his contrast between the actual and his ideal, which contrast is missing from Knight's theory.

Speculation and Monetarism

Keynes's speculators interact in a way that is unpredictable and yet ultimately automatic and mechanical, *causa essendi* without *causa cognoscendi*. What they do is automatic in the sense that their action is caused by objective factors, yet paradoxically this very automaticity exaggerates the fluidity and unpredictability of economic affairs. It is Keynes's objective chance at work, or the Errant Necessity of the Greeks. Their combination of the inevitable with the unpredictable expresses well the sense of Keynes's concept of economic behaviour.

Because of the extensive meaning that Keynes gave to speculation, it cannot be separated from his economic theory in general. In Keynes's sense probably most of modern economic behaviour is speculative. By way of contrast, Milton Friedman makes speculation the topic of an essay which shows that this peripheral subject—for in the main it may be bypassed—does not disturb the efficiency and stability of market equilibrium. Keynes made speculation the centre-piece of his economic theory, the subject of some of his most brilliant eloquence. Speculation is his *reductio ad absurdum* of the doctrine that the benefits of all are best met through the free play of individual desires.

According to Friedman, there is no logical proof that speculation is destabilizing. In his essay on speculation, he says that if speculation is akin to casino gambling, that is only a proof of its desirability, since people pay good money for their pleasures at the gambling house (Friedman 1960/1969:288–9). All that society can ask is that the market should be freely able to determine its optimal level of speculation, according to the costs and benefits seen by each person.

The monetarists do not need to canvas whether speculation affects their natural rate of unemployment, because even if unemployment were increased by speculation, the new natural rate of unemployment would remain the 'natural' rate. The argument is logical given its assumptions concerning economic rationality, but it is these assumptions that Keynes challenged. There is nothing 'natural', meaning nothing determinate or regular, in Keynes's economic theories because economic decisions, being arbitrary in origin and effect, are part of the blind processes of objective chance. Keynes and the monetarists both believe that the economic ideal and rational action are intertwined, but they differ over the meaning of rationality.

Notes to Chapter 5

1. Keynes's endorsement of the M–C–M' process shows a parallel between his ethics and those of Marx, but there is also a difference. Marx acknowledged that he drew the concept from Aristotle—see *Capital*, I, Pt. 2, iv, 152. The M–C–M' psychology is what Aristotle called chrematistic behaviour, for the purpose of unlimited money-making, whereas C–M–C' is economic behaviour, to acquire commodities for other purposes. The unlimited character of chrematistic meant, according to Aristotle, that it was unnatural.

   Marx gave Aristotle's distinction a social character; the capitalist is a *rational* miser, even though his chrematistic actions destabilize the economy. Keynes returned to an individualist notion; purposiveness is irrational for the individual, but it is not destructive in the economy, and it may actually be beneficial, provided a different morality prevails in politics.
2. Joan Robinson said that the Keynesian revolution 'lay in the change from the principles of rational choice [profit-maximizing] to the problems of decisions based on guesswork and convention' (Robinson 1980b:3).
3. See Dow and Dow (1985:60): Keynes 'conformed more to what, for want of a better term, we may call the "Babylonian" mode. In line with this view, "purple passages" in the *General Theory*, including the term animal spirits, were an integral part of his attempt to communicate and persuade.' Elsewhere the authors also suggest that animal spirits came from the Greek tradition.
4. To anticipate Chapter 9, Keynes believed that there was scope for creativity in the *political* field. Both Keynes and Knight believed that the political problem required that democracy should be supplemented by the abilities that had been (in Knight's case still were) in the sphere of business. 'The case of the ultimate entrepreneur, dealing with and knowing men rather than things, suggests again the analogous political problem [which was to give democracy the veto power and otherwise to keep it in the background]. The progress of democracy toward intelligent efficiency seems to depend upon a tendency for the ultimate sovereign, the electorate, to centre its attention on the selection of competent agents, leaving to them the actual formulation of policies and conduct of affairs' (Knight 1921:302).

6

Other Accounts of Keynesian Ethics and Uncertainty

> Know'st not at this stale time
> That shaken and unshaken are alike
> But demonstrations from the Back of Things?
>
> Thomas Hardy, *The Dynasts*

Keynes regarded economics and politics as aspects of an extended process of reason based upon a coherent but pre-modern ethics. For a variety of reasons, including his pragmatism, his opposition to formalistic economic theory, and the nuances of 'Keynes-neutral' policies, his philosophy has been misunderstood. The usual picture is the Keynes who 'lacked the scruple of a scholar', a butterfly who hovered brilliantly over the world of thought without alighting. Yet the usual picture has no foundation except frequent reiteration. A much more real Keynes could be drawn as a composite from authoritative sources—the neo-Keynesian insistence that Keynes was not a consequentialist; Skidelsky on the influence of Moore but the abandonment of the conventions; Harrod on Keynes's general idealism; and Hutchison on his rational ethics.[1] None the less, even these authors have subscribed to the butterfly story, despite the long apprenticeship that Keynes served in moral and political philosophy.

Theories of Keynes's Ethics

Harrod was in the best position to give an informed account of Keynes's philosophy and its influence on his economics. Yet although it is possible, for reasons which will become apparent, that Harrod understood Keynes in much the same terms as mine, he portrayed Keynes as a conventional modern economist.

He acknowledged no influence of Moore except through the *Treatise of Probability*; he played down the influence of Moore even on the *Treatise*; he disparaged the *Treatise* as a purely speculative work without practical significance;[2] and he implied, though without saying so, that Keynes was a positivist and a utilitarian economist (Harrod 1951:134).

The manner in which Harrod exorcized Moore from the *Treatise* is an instructive example:

> Moore's influence . . . was very general in character. It was natural for Keynes to express indebtedness [to Moore] in his preface [to the *Treatise on Probability*] considering the very high regard, approaching veneration, which he felt for Moore. The Memoir Club statement concerning the 'important contributory cause' [of Moore on Keynes] is not very convincing, because it is a platitude that right conduct must often depend on a balance of probabilities. (Harrod 1951:652)

The reader might well conclude that Keynes had learnt, from Moore, that right conduct depends upon a balance of the probabilities, and that Keynes had said so in his Memoir Club statement (later published as 'My Early Beliefs'). In fact, neither Moore nor Keynes ever held such a theory, which would be inconsistent with their stress on organic unities and unquantifiable uncertainty. This supposed 'platitude' was an error in Keynes's eyes, as he said at length in VIII:334 *et seq.* and there is nothing in the Memoir Club statement that even hints otherwise (see especially X:445).

The reader has been misled, but he would be misled even further by Harrod's next sentence. If there *is* uncertainty, then the best motives for action could be either to follow the social rules (Moore) or to follow an intuitable duty (Keynes). Harrod rejected Keynes's solution to uncertainty, without advising the reader that Keynes was the one being rejected.

> It must be admitted, however, that Moore's ethic makes the problems of uncertainty and probability more prominent than does an ethic which allows for an intuitable duty, for by the latter a course of action can be known for certain to be a duty even if some of its consequences are uncertain; this is impossible on Moore's view. (Harrod, 1951:652)

Now Moore is back; this sentence invokes Moore to refute Keynes without admitting that Keynes had the philosophy at issue.

Presumably Moore's religion was bad enough, but Keynes's development of an ethical system out of it was even worse. Skidelsky has accused Harrod of playing down Moore to protect Keynes's reputation, because Moore's Bloomsbury disciples were sexually unorthodox bohemians. Perhaps Harrod also had a larger, if equally wrong-headed, aim; to protect Keynesian economics by hiding its suspect archaic roots. In any event, the effect was that Keynes's economics was cut off from his philosophy of probability. This was the first step which turned Keynes into a fragmentary thinker, without a unified system of thought.

The next step cut off Keynes's ethics from his theory of probability. Although Harrod stopped short of calling Keynes a utilitarian, he permitted and encouraged such an interpretation, and R. B. Braithwaite gave it a stamp of authority. Braithwaite (1975:242) admitted that he was surprised by the attack on Bentham in 'My Early Beliefs', but he assumed that Keynes had misrepresented his own philosophy. Believing that 'Keynes was brought up in, and never departed from, a consequentialist moral philosophy', Braithwaite gave no analytical reason for supposing that Keynes misrepresented his own philosophy, and addressed only the psychological question of why Keynes should have said something he did not really believe.

To summarize the argument, Braithwaite compared Keynes to a Christian who discards his religion but unthinkingly retains Christian behaviour in his private life; Keynes discarded Benthamism as a philosophy but was a consequentialist in action. Keynes, he said, was not fully serious about his criticism of Bentham, because he was debunking Sidgwick and *his* utilitarian theories for personal reasons. Keynes's attack was so vehement because he was trying to play the iconoclast and dazzle the younger generation to whom he first read his essay:

My explanation, perhaps, does not account for the violence of Keynes' invective against the 'Benthamite tradition'—the worm which has been gnawing at the insides of modern civilization and is responsible for its present moral decay . . . I suspect that Keynes said this, and connected Benthamism to Marxism a few sentences later, chiefly *pour épater les jeunes*. (Braithwaite 1975:244)

These arguments, which as I have said are more psychological than philosophical, are inadequate because throughout his life Keynes made many attacks on both utilitarianism and Benthamism. I have mentioned that Keynes opted for organic unities rather than utilitarianism in 'A Theory of Beauty', and that he criticized the utilitarian theory of probability in the *Treatise on Probability*. There are side-swipes in his biographical essays: 'How disappointing are the fruits, now that we have them, of the bright idea of reducing Economics to a mathematical application of the hedonistic calculus of Bentham!' (X:184). And in X:260 Keynes described utilitarianism as an outmoded doctrine, although 'we still trust the superstructure [of economics] without exploring too thoroughly the soundness of the original [utilitarian] foundations'. After the *General Theory* he attacked Benthamism as the false moral philosophy which underlay classical economics:

I sum up, therefore, the main grounds of my departure [from classical economics] as follows:
(1) The orthodox theory assumes that we have a knowledge of the future of a kind quite different from that which we actually possess. This false rationalization follows the lines of the Benthamite calculus. The hypothesis of a calculable future leads to a wrong interpretation of the principles of behaviour which the need for action compels us to adopt. (XIV:122)

As this passage indicates, Keynes did not deny that people would try to act as utilitarians; this is the element of truth in the picture of Keynes as a utilitarian. However, he believed that their attempts to do so required a 'false rationalization' because of uncertainty and organic unities, or that rational self-interest was not necessarily rational after all.

Skidelsky accepted that Keynes was a consequentialist, even though he took Harrod to task for leaving Moore out of the story. But Keynes as a consequentialist does not make sense; and so Skidelsky presented a Keynes whose thought, although immersed in philosophy, had to be accounted for in terms of his personal and social background. He began by enlisting the support of the eminent historian of economic analysis, Joseph Schumpeter, who said that there is a suggestive link between Keynes's 'childless vision' and his emphasis on uncertainty and the short run; and he pointed out that, although in economics it is not done to give details of the lives of authors, in the literary tradition it has been common. Keynes's biography holds the key to his vision, because 'philosophy provided the foundation of Keynes' life' (Skidelsky 1983:133), and life influences thought. This may well be so. In general, Skidelsky has highlighted the significance of Keynes's early writings, for which economists are indebted to him, and I suggest that their discovery may be as significant as the discovery of the early writings of Marx. I have followed here two of his themes, namely, that Keynes had a mental outlook which has virtually disappeared; and that within this outlook Keynes rejected a philosophy of following conventions, and yet connected true beliefs and action. Nevertheless, my concern is not biographical, but to show that there was a direct and *analytical* relation between Keynes's ethics and his economics and politics.

Schumpeter was an arch positivist who assumed away the possibility of such an analytical relation. Admittedly, he insisted that some vision underlies each economic theory, and he thought that Keynes's economics were based on a consistent vision,[3] points with which I do agree in the abstract. However, by a vision Schumpeter meant a set of personal and social circumstances, which in Keynes's instance were the short-run childless outlook and concern for an arteriosclerotic English economy (Schumpeter 1954:1171). 'Philosophy in any technical sense of the term is constitutionally unable to influence economic analysis and actually has not influenced it', he wrote in the preface to his *History of Economic Analysis* (1954:32). Leaving aside his particular account of Keynes's vision, I am at odds with a method which by definition and without argument excludes Keynes's ethics and philosophy of probability from his economic theories.

Skidelsky does not endorse such a restrictive approach in principle, but in practice he takes the Schumpeterian road. He interprets Moore as a temporary halting post on the way to complete valuelessness and the disintegration of the Victorian world view. Moore was disenchanted with Bentham and the utilitarians and said that, instead of making utility the purpose of life, people should aim at truth, beauty and love. Keynes later admitted that he followed Moore and understood truth, beauty and love in an excessively aesthetic way; Skidelsky adds on Keynes's behalf that he also understood love in a sensual way.

Keynes later admitted that he had overlooked Chapter 5 in Moore's *Principia Ethica*, the chapter that defended conventional morality. There Moore says that practical situations are so complex, and the chain of consequences is so extended and uncertain, that it is simply impossible in most cases to make rational decisions. Moore concluded that usually the best course is to simply follow convention and be moral, which was too Victorian a solution for Keynes.

We may interpret Skidelsky as saying that Keynes could not fully follow Moore because there was an unresolved duality in Moore. Since it is not obvious what relevance the mind states of truth, beauty and love have to the economic and political problems of the day, Moore had not solved the problem of valuelessness at all. Rather, he had only stated the existential problem in a new way, because there was still a chasm between values and what should be done in practice. Moore was looking for absolutes with a Victorian mentality, but his positive achievement was to unshackle ethics from conventional morality, so that rational ethics could never take Victorian morality seriously again.

Familiarity with Keynes's writings soon shows that the story of Keynes the immoralist does not make sense either. Skidelsky says that at first Keynes rejected conventions and lived as a sybarite. Yet, although initially Moore's ethics gave Keynes a licence to overthrow values and live as a free spirit, an ambivalence also eventually came to infect Keynes. The First World War was a watershed. Keynes became despairing of the senselessness and stupidity of the war. He turned back to the Victorian values which Moore had been unable either to eradicate or genuinely to justify. Skidelsky concludes:

> When belief in God waned they [Keynes and his group] could not help but feel that the moral capital which sustained the accumulation of economic capital had been severely depleted. . . . The vanished nineteenth-century certainties seemed curiously comforting in retrospect. . . . In the last resort Keynes' post-war fear for the future of capitalism was profoundly influenced by the Victorian fear of a godless society. The prospect of civilization briefly opened up by Moore's *Principia Ethica* had receded over the horizon. The rest of Keynes' life was spent in trying to bring it back into sight. (Skidelsky 1983:402)

I have said that according to Harrod Keynes accepted the

Cambridge ideals of 'unworldliness, truth, and other absolute
values'. Skidelsky successfully shows that Harrod left out the
earthy part of the biographical story, but Skidelsky in turn
omitted the idealist part of the story. To give some notion of the
thrust of Skidelsky's biography, if it were the only one possible,
then, far from being unworldly, Keynes's vision could be
resolved into fear and desire, coloured by his social and cultural
environment. Even though it was expressed in philosophical
terms, the seeming enigmatic quality in Keynes's thought, his
stature as a philosopher-king among economists, would be
dissolved, and Keynes would be yet another worldly philosopher
as economists tend to be.

   Without defending Keynes, and without disputing the merits
of a biographical approach, it alone does not tell the full story,
especially when Skidelsky omits Keynes's own interpretation of
his early views. Keynes did not think at all that his theories were
based upon an oscillation between values and valuelessness, but
he believed that he had progressed towards greater depth and
intellectual clarity. In 'My Early Beliefs' Keynes gave a reason
why his ideas developed in a particular direction, and explained
the superficial element in some of his early ideas. This is not
necessarily to say that Keynes interpreted his own philosophy
correctly, but it is to suggest that by leaving out these reasons
Skidelsky too implicitly assumed away a possible logical link
between economics and the vision.

Keynes's Theory of Uncertainty

This book has stressed the close relationship between Keynes's
ethics and his theory of uncertainty, and yet when we pass from
ethics to the economics of uncertainty the exegetical scene
entirely changes. Among economists, the prevailing view is that
Keynes was not a utilitarian, nor a consequentialist or economic
maximizer, but that to the contrary he re-routed economics *away
from* its consequentialism.

   Yet, although there is general agreement about what Keynes
did not say (consequentialism), there are two different accounts
of what he did. One is the subjectivist interpretation of G. L. S.
Shackle, that Keynes, believing that economic calculation is

impossible, concluded that everything must depend on subjective preferences and good states of mind. The other is the neo-Keynesian account, that Keynes thought economic behaviour can only be based on conformity to conventional social ideas; and it is noteworthy that Joan Robinson's *Accumulation of Capital* (1958) opens with a story about robins, the moral being that the economy is just an elaboration on the (conventional) birds.

Shackle believes that Keynesian uncertainty is purely subjective, and Tony Lawson, defending the neo-Keynesian line, argues that it is purely objective. I will criticize both of their accounts to support my own theory, that Keynesian uncertainty is analogous to Keynesian ethics: there is an objective ideal, but common behaviour is subjective. I will confine myself to the technical question of whether Shackle and Lawson are right to claim Keynes's authority for their ideas, rather than considering whether these ideas are valuable in themselves. The reader should also be aware that uncertainty is one of those abstract words that have political implications. Professor Shackle believes that his version of uncertainty supports a case for *laissez-faire*, and Dr Lawson believes that considerations of uncertainty support socialist economics. (Neither Lawson nor Shackle considers what Keynes's own politics might be, but I will show below that Keynes's economics of uncertainty corresponds to his own political ideals.)

I will argue that, although Shackle and Lawson are on opposite sides of the political fence, they both apply the materialist interpretation of Keynes, which I argue, throughout this book, is a main reason why Keynes has been misunderstood. Therefore, although I acknowledge that Shackle and Lawson both offer valuable insights, I accuse them of the common error of overlooking Keynes's idealism.

Professor Shackle has the more obvious argument, developed at much greater length, and his books are well known. He begins from Keynes's argument that investors do not act rationally. In his book *Keynesian Kaleidics*, he comments on the passage (XIV:115) from Keynes, quoted in Chapter 5, to the effect that 'behaviour based on a flimsy foundation is liable to sudden and violent changes':

It has long appeared to me that Keynes' expositors, commentators and critics either contrive, for the sake of their peace of mind, to leave this passage unread, or else they turn aside as men who have looked over the edge into the abyss and must endeavour to blot this dreadful vision from their mind. (Shackle 1974:38)

I am sympathetic with this point and with the argument that Keynes rejected the assumption of rational economic man. Yet, despite this important agreement, Shackle's interpretation of Keynes is otherwise opposite to my own, for although Shackle does not refer to David Hume, he interprets Keynes to have Hume's position. Whereas I say that Keynes rejected the rationality of economic man and turned to another concept of rationality, Shackle does not recognize that there *is* any other sort. Shackle supports the Austrian doctrine of subjectivism, so called because it believes that all economic decisions are, and can only be, entirely subjective. He takes Hume's view that value judgements have no rational basis, and arise only through the emotions, and he extends this to say that probability judgements also have only a subjective basis. The argument is that a probability judgement, like a value judgement, is not based upon strict logical premises. Just as a car cannot pass over a bridge with one missing span, Shackle says, a probabilistic argument cannot lead to a genuine conclusion,[4] and emotion must step in if a conclusion is to be reached.

I think that what Keynes had in mind is an aspect of what elsewhere I have ventured to call his kaleidic account of the economic process of history . . . the view that men are conscious of their essential and irremediable state of un-knowledge and that they usually suppress this awareness in the interest of avoiding a paralysis of action; but that from time to time they succumb to its abiding mockery and menace, and withdraw from the field. (Shackle 1974:42)

Shackle believes that, since all probability statements are subjective, we can either deceive ourselves and act out our deceptions, or we can be rational, play Hamlet and sit in a state of paralysis. The rational man finds that the native hue of his active resolution is sicklied over with the pale cast of thought. This is pure Hume, but Shackle fathers his idea on Keynes, which is to say that he fathers the subjective theory of probability on its greatest antagonist and the founder of the opposite, which is the logical theory of probability. These two theories are opposites over the central issue, which is whether it is possible to act rationally under conditions of probability and uncertainty, but in various ways Professor Shackle slurs over the differences. For example, he proposes what he calls an 'extension' of Keynes's theory in the *Treatise on Probability*, which has the effect of wrongly representing that the logical theory of probability is akin to the subjectivist version (Shackle 1974:388). In another instance he writes: 'Keynes speaks *passim* of degrees of rational belief. Since I cannot accept his interpretation of this phrase I have here evaded the issue . . .' (Shackle 1974:41), which in general he does by denying that Keynes had a concept of rational belief. Keynes often says that actions and beliefs can be rational ('We should not conclude from this that everything depends upon waves of irrational psychology', *GT*:162), to which Shackle responds by saying that Keynes was logically inconsistent.

In terms of Shackle's metaphor, the Keynes of the *Treatise on Probability* could retort that the mind *can* leap over the missing span by means of intuitive analogies, and arrive at a conclusion that would be more likely than any other (even if it cannot reach a conclusion that is more likely than not). According to the *Treatise*, 'our logic is concerned with drawing conclusions by series of steps . . . from a limited body of premises', and 'in the actual exercise of reason we do not wait on certainty, or deem it irrational to depend on a doubtful argument' (VIII:3). If it is said that in the *General Theory* Keynes effectively excluded analogies when he assumed utter uncertainty, he nevertheless believed it possible to be rational without crossing over the bridge, that the rational basis of action is not necessarily on the far side of a chain of logical syllogisms. When there is radical uncertainty, then the rationality of motives rather than ends comes into play.

Professor Shackle defends his interpretation of Keynes by saying that Keynes 'did not understand the full reach of his own conclusions' (Shackle 1972:429), and that Keynes 'spared the reader' (p. 333). But if Keynes did spare the reader, he would stand accused of silently abandoning not only his theory of probability but, much worse, his commitment to ruthless truth-telling. Keynes would have taken an about-turn in his whole philosophy and everything that followed from it. To give only one instance, he would have been obliged to abandon his interventionist economics in favour of a radical non-interventionist stand, because if he really believed that no rational response to uncertainty is possible, then the merit of controlling the economy is nil; complete uncertainty leads to nihilism in controlling the economy as in everything else. Professor Shackle was well aware of this conclusion, but if Keynes knew it and spared the reader—even worse, if he knew it and still disputed the merits of economic control with von Hayek—then he would have been guilty of a combination of intellectual confusion and moral cowardice, because Keynes's philosophy should lead to Austrian subjectivism and extreme *laissez-faire*.

Given, however, that it is possible to interpret Keynes's philosophy as being logically consistent, it is more likely that Professor Shackle has been misled. There are misleading concordances between Keynes and subjectivism which arise because they are both radical, or tend to go to the roots of the problem of uncertainty. Keynes and Hume both believed that it was not possible to draw *strict* logical deductions about probabilistic and uncertain situations. They were agreed in opposing those who pass too superficially from probabilistic data to a conclusion— who refuse to look into the abyss. They also both believed that probability judgements and value judgements had the same status—the validity of either sort of judgement stood or fell with the validity of the other.

But there are very pronounced differences, which arise because Keynes was a philosopher of action whereas Hume was a philosopher of science. One is that Keynes as a philosopher of action did not think that strict logic was necessary to reach a reasonable conclusion, because he thought (and said) that demonstrable reasoning is only a special instance of probabilistic reasoning; another is that Keynes rejected the idea that value judgements are based only upon the imagination, which means that he rejected subjectivism. Shackle does not recognize these dimensions of Keynes's thinking, much less analyse their significance, but they permeate every aspect of Keynes's politics and economics.

Carabelli's account of a subjective Keynes (Carabelli 1985a) is more sophisticated than the Shackle account, but it is open to similar objections. Unlike Shackle, Carabelli portrays Keynes as only ultimately, rather than entirely, nihilistic. But like Shackle, she too overlooks Moore and dismisses the logical theory of probability—'The "logicist" interpretation of Keynes' theory [of probability] is thus probably based on a hasty reading of Keynes' text' (p. 166). None the less, Keynes insisted that his theory was the logical theory of probability, as distinct from the ultimately subjective theory she attributes to him; and when Carabelli refers to Keynes's 'logic of opinion rather than of truth' (p. 167), she too attributes to Keynes not his own ideas, but the philosophy of David Hume.

Dr Lawson has written only one article on uncertainty, but it is significant as the only attempt to reconcile the *Treatise on Probability* with neo-Keynesian economics. His is by no means an easy position to maintain, because the *Treatise* is more obviously imbued with the spirit of Moore, Locke and the Greeks than with Ricardo and Marx. Nevertheless, Lawson imputes a socialist morality to Keynes, who, he says, thought that investors are rational because they usually follow the social rules instead of being calculating profit-maximizers. The critical assumption (shades of Skidelsky) is that Keynes thought that being rational meant following the social rules. This very dubious point granted, Dr Lawson's argument then proceeds easily. In the *Treatise on Probability*, Keynes said that probability is a logical relation. In the *General Theory* he says that when faced with uncertainty the investors follow the conventional rules when deciding whether to invest. Bringing the argument together, Lawson is able to deduce that Keynes's theory of uncertainty is only about *logical* probability. Keynes, says Dr Lawson (1985:914), 'appears to maintain a consistent viewpoint over a span of thirty years'; i.e., uncertainty is a logical state, and is no different from probability.

Lawson does not mention G. E. Moore, but his argument turns Keynes's relation to Moore upside down. To recall Chapter 3, Keynes rejected Moore's morality, which was following the social rules, and adopted his religion, which meant observing only the transcendental rules. This is why Keynes began to write the *Treatise on Probability* in the first place. When Lawson says that Keynes thought it rational to follow the conventions, he attributes to Keynes the idea that Keynes initially wrote to refute. Reason requires, as Keynes's 'Theory of Beauty' said, that we 'shake off the cloud of convention'.

Lawson has Keynes following Moore's morality rather than his religion.

Keynes did not maintain a fully consistent view over the decades in one critical respect. According to the *Treatise on Probability*, the human mind exercises a power of rational intuition, whereas in the *General Theory* investors are not rational. This is the obvious and glaring difference between the *Treatise on Probability* and the *General Theory*. 'In estimating the prospects for investment, we must have regard therefore, to the nerves and hysteria and even the digestions and reactions to the weather of those upon whose spontaneous activity it largely depends' (*GT*:162): this is typical *General Theory*, and is simply not about rational investors. Nor is there any passage like this in the *Treatise on Probability*.

I agree that there is some consistency in Keynes over the years, but by correctly drawing attention to it Lawson has overstated it. If Keynes had really not changed his ideas at all over thirty years, the investors in the *General Theory* would not have followed the social conventions: they would have followed their logical intuitions about the future, based on the power of the intuitive mind to perceive by analogies and on the organic nature of goodness and the Universe. There would not have been a *General Theory*, much less a logical interpretation of uncertainty.

I also agree with Lawson that Professor Shackle has drawn a picture of entire subjectivity whereas Keynes meant to include reason in the picture, and that there is a relation between probability and uncertainty. However, it is the *criterion* of rational behaviour, not the *prevalence* of rational behaviour, that carries over. Because Shackle and Lawson both overlook Keynes's distinction between the common action and the rational ideal, they each have a different half of the truth. Shackle makes a system only out of the common action, and Lawson makes one out of the rational ideal.

In conclusion, the most prominent accounts of Keynes's theories of ethics and uncertainty are mutually inconsistent; and in particular, the theories of Braithwaite and Skidelsky are inconsistent with the probabilistic accounts of the economists, which in turn are at odds among themselves. In addition, they are all inconsistent with what Keynes actually said on some point of philosophical substance, and require supplementary arguments, again at odds among themselves, that Keynes did not mean what he said. However, these accounts can be reconciled, and an element of partial truth found in each, if we draw a different picture of Keynes that recognizes his idealism. The ideal is neither to follow the conventions nor to breach them, neither to maximize utility nor to be utterly subjective. It is not even consequentialist in the usual sense, but involves a rational, if intuitive, evaluation of the interaction between facts and the categories of good and evil.

Notes to Chapter 6

1. Because of the economics of uncertainty, economists have often speculated that Keynes was not a utilitarian. But only T. W. Hutchison has declared that Keynes had a rational ethics based on Moore's religion: 'Thus for Keynes, the belief in progress was buttressed by an ardent belief in "rationality". Though by 1938 he still held that his early beliefs, or "this religion of ours", remained "nearer the truth than any other that I know", Keynes had come to regard this "rationalist" tenet as superficial and misconceived—though he admitted that he was still dominated by it' (Hutchison 1981:74). Hutchison explained Keynes's approach to economic *policy* in terms of his religion—it gave Keynes reason to want to be the driver of the economy and not just the engineer. However, Hutchison did not connect ethics and probability, and so he did not trace the influence of Keynes's religion on his formal economic *theories*.
2. Harrod dismissed the *Treatise on Probability* as an exercise in pure logic, conceding only that Keynes's 'fundamental logic speculations cannot be ruled out as inevitably of no practical use', since someone might find a role for them when 'the next great simplifying hypothesis' comes along (Harrod 1951:134). Evidently he did not regard the next great simplifying hypothesis as Keynes's own theory of uncertainty.
3. 'The whole period between 1919 and 1936 was then spent in attempts, first unsuccessful, then increasingly successful, at implementing the particular vision . . . that was fixed in Keynes' mind by 1919 at the latest' (Schumpeter 1954:42).
4. '"Rationality" is an empty and idle term until the data available to the individual are specified. If they are incorrect, what is the good of his taking action which would be rational if they were correct? If they are essentially incomplete, conduct which assumes them to be sufficient may plunge to disaster through the gaps of knowledge

which it has ignored. For the traveller in the dusk, a bridge with a missing span is worse than merely useless' (Shackle 1972:37).

Shackle implies wrongly that Keynes subscribed to this analogy (p. 391).

7

Economics of Transitoriness

Those who suggest that the doctrine of universal flux was
not new, are, I feel, unconscious witnesses to Heraclitus'
originality; for they fail now, after 2,400 years, to grasp his
main point. They do not see the difference between a flux or
circulation *within* a vessel or an edifice or a cosmic
framework, i.e. *within a totality of things* (part of the
Heraclitean theory can indeed be understood in this way,
but only that part of it which is not very original), and a
universal flux which embraces everything, even the vessel,
the framework itself and which is described by Heraclitus'
denial of the existence of any fixed thing whatever.

Slightly abridged from K. Popper,
The Open Society and Its Enemies

Keynes's duality of heaven and earth, of ideals and the flux, was
translated into his formal economics, and especially into the
General Theory. Corresponding to the sphere of ideals was an
economic yardstick, a new definition of economic rationality
which highlighted the flux. Corresponding to the flux was a
centreless economy, the economy of uncertainty and change.
'Enterprise becomes the bubble on a whirlpool of speculation', he
wrote in the *General Theory*, and compared the investment
decision to a newspaper competition in which the competitors
have to guess what the other competitors are guessing what the
others are guessing, to the *n*th degree.

The links between Keynes's philosophy and his formal
economics have been obscured because the Keynesians have all
simply omitted the connecting theory. Keynes himself declared
these links—the monetary theory of interest and the new theory
of value—to be central, but from the beginning they were
omitted because they made no sense to the Keynesians. The
General Theory is not a general scientific theory, as science is

usua'lly understood, and did not pretend to be. It was a conscious return to the pre-classical traditions, which understood economics as an art, based on common sense subject to the principles of reason:

What I want is to do justice to schools of thought which the classicals have treated as imbecile for the last hundred years and, above all, to show that I am not really being so great an innovator, except as against the classical school, but have important predecessors and am returning to an age-long tradition of common sense. (XIII:552)

The harmony of Keynes's earlier ideas with his economics was accomplished only over time. He stood on the boundary of known economic thought in the *Tract on Monetary Reform*; he was wide of both sides of the mark in the *Treatise on Money*. Only the *General Theory* presented a true moral science of economics, for it is in the preface to that work that Keynes first referred to economics as a moral science.

Economic Indeterminancy

The theme that unites Keynes's macroeconomic and monetary writings, from the *Tract on Monetary Reform* to the *Treatise on Money* and the *General Theory*, is the indeterminancy of the economy; but the meaning of indeterminancy evolved over time. In the *Tract*, Keynes accepted the quantity theory of money, according to which the absolute price level is set by the quantity of money in the long run, and observed that in the long run we are all dead. In the short run we are in the tempest of events, and it does not help much to know that eventually the ocean will be flat again, and eventually prices will once more be proportional to money. Even so, Keynes also went beyond this, suggesting that even the eventual level of the economic ocean depends upon the nature of the tempest. A change in the money supply would change not only the price level, but also the monetary habits of the public, as people sought to make gains or avoid loss, and this would lead to a new equilibrium:

Thus after, during, and (so far as the change is anticipated) before a change in the value of money, there will be some reaction on the velocity of money, with the result that the change in the value of the price level, at least temporarily and perhaps permanently (since habits and practices, once changed, will not revert to exactly their old shape), will not be precisely in proportion to the change in money. (IV:66–7) (For clarity I have translated Keynes's algebraic symbols in the above passage into words.)

Therefore, in the interests of price stability the authorities should offset any major movement around the equilibrium price level, so that there will be expectations of a norm of price stability.

It is one of the objects of this book to urge that the best way to cure this mortal disease of individualism is to provide that there shall never exist any confident expectation either that prices generally are going to fall or that they are going to rise; and also that there shall be no serious risk that a movement, if it does occur, will be a big one. (IV:35)

Keynes was still thinking in terms of economic equilibrium. By bringing in changing expectations, he was turning towards a way of thinking that eventually would dispense with equilibrium, but in the *Tract* the emphasis was on establishing economic rules within which the principle of indifference would artificially apply.

Next, in the *Treatise on Money*, Keynes still accepted that a natural (equilibrium) rate of interest was set in the long run by the real productive forces in the economy; but he rejected the determinateness of prices, even in the long run. In particular, he disputed the notion that if one set of prices went up, with the quantity of money remaining constant, then another set of prices must go down, like two buckets rising and falling in a well. Instead, Keynes argued that the quantity theory of money was inadequate because prices depended upon expectations and other forces outside the economic system.

However, he denied the possibility of a determinate explanation for prices in two different senses. In one sense,

I was trying to illustrate the point that the old quantity notions are incapable of leading us to the price level of output, by pointing out that all or any of the variables occurring in the quantity equation might be unchanged and yet the price level of output might be changed. In other words, not only does the price level of output not occur explicitly in the old quantity equation, but it is not even a function of those variables which do occur in it. (XIII:231)

In the other sense, in a passage that particularly influenced G. L. S. Shackle,

We must not argue . . . that an expansion of the currency influences relative prices in the same way as the translation of the earth through space affects the relative position of the objects on its surface. The effect of moving a kaleidoscope on the coloured pieces of glass within is almost a better metaphor for the influence of monetary changes on price levels. (V:81)

The first quotation raises a point of theory, the second a point of method. The first is part of Keynes's attempt to devise a new theory of prices, based on total demand in the economy rather than the quantity theory of money; the second says that no theory of prices is really possible. The *Treatise on Money* revolves around two unreconciled conceptions, one of which is that of Keynes the classical economist, locked in the abstract prison of equilibrium but trying to forge analytical tools of escape, and the other of which is that of Keynes the free wanderer in the fluid probabilistic world, but a disembodied spirit looking for an economic theory. Each conception is worked out in a separate section of the book. The free wanderer Keynes is in Section II, which implicitly draws on objective chance, and the invalidity of the principle of indifference, from the *Treatise on Probability*. The restless classical Keynes is in Section III, where new 'fundamental equations' are formulated in terms of savings and investment instead of the old quantity theory of money.

Keynes saw no relation between these two sections, and in the preface to the *Treatise* he opted for what would become the mechanics of the *General Theory*, rather than what would become its spirit. He wrote that Section III was 'a novel approach to the fundamental problems of monetary theory', whereas, by comparison, Section II was a long 'quasi-digression' which he suggested could perhaps be omitted by the reader. Yet this supposedly superfluous digression was to form the basis of Shackle's theories of uncertainty; Section II is the missing link between economics and probability, and, being unconstrained by formal economic analysis, its method is more radical than that of the *General Theory*.

The Section III tool of escape, which Keynes formulated while sitting in the Ricardian prison, and which would be ready for later use, was savings and investment analysis. The argument was that *laissez-faire* cannot be a perfectly self-adusting system because of the possibility that money will be hoarded. The classical theory had not taken hoarding into account: according to classical theory, all money saved was supposed to be invested, which was why savings were supposedly equal to investment, and why supply always created its own demand. According to the *Treatise on Money*, however, saving was separate from, and unrelated to, the hoarding of money. Saving meant not consuming commodities, hoarding meant withdrawing money from circulation, and there was no necessary relation between the two. An investor could shuffle his investment portfolio of assets towards money without intending to reduce his consumption. If money was suddenly hoarded there could be a shortfall in investment compared with saving, and the economy could get into disequilibrium.

Although we know with hindsight that this is suggestive of the *General Theory*, Keynes still thought in classical terms. He did not yet consider that hoarding might arise out of an irrational and volatile M–C–M′ psychology. He meant to extend classical economics, to de-emphasize the equilibrium point in favour of the dynamic path to equilibrium. Because the quantity theory of money assumed that prices were always proportional to the money supply, it was only an equilibrium equation that could not analyse the transitional path. Keynes conceived a new, more fundamental system, beginning from the labour theory of value, which would somehow bring in the dynamics of the economy. 'For the labour power of money and the purchasing power of money are fundamental in a sense in which the price levels based on other types of expenditures are not.' However, his value theory played no role in Section III.

The *Treatise on Money* did not intend to refute classical economics, as the *General Theory* did. To judge by Section III alone, the foremost classical economist of Keynes's time, the most consciously classical economist, was Keynes himself. He accepted without equivocation that there was a long-run natural rate of interest, based on the productivity of capital, which was equilibrium. Departures from the natural rate would, as in the typical classical theory, lead to a different level of prices, the quantities of capital and labour employed being implicitly assumed constant.

In Section II, in the process of refuting the quantity theory of money, Keynes made points that implicitly refuted his own classical tendencies. The principle of indifference in that section is not named, but the concept is under attack. Jevons, Cournot and Edgeworth had conceived an ideal or 'intrinsic' value of money which they thought could be found by selecting the correct index of prices to be used as a deflator. Keynes went past a response to this idea, which today is not very plausible anyway, to analyse the nature of economic causation. If the principle of indifference cannot validly be assumed, and objective chance applies, then there is no average or normal set of prices in the economy.

Nevertheless I venture to maintain that such ideas, which I have endeavoured to expound above as fairly and as plausibly as I can, are root-and-branch erroneous. The 'errors of observation', the 'faulty shots aimed at a single bull's eye' conception of the index number of prices, Edgeworth's 'objective mean variation of general prices', is the result of a confusion of thought. There is no bull's eye. There is no moving but unique centre, to be called the general price level or the objective mean variation of general prices, round which are scattered the moving price levels of individual things. There are all the various, quite definite, conceptions of price-levels of composite commodities appropriate for various purposes and inquiries which have been scheduled above, and many others too. There is nothing else. Jevons was pursuing a mirage. (V:76–7)

This is not only an argument about index numbers, because it could lead to a rejection of the equilibrium concept itself, and Keynes unambiguously took the further step. If it is invalid to assume that deviations in observation will cancel out and leave a perfect statistic, then it is equally invalid to assume that deviations in actual prices can be cancelled out to leave a concept of economic equilibrium. Indeed, one of the reasons why there is assumed to be a perfect index number is that we assume the normal theory of value:

This [erroneous] notion has flourished under a combination of influences. In the first place the influence of the 'normal' theory of value has encouraged a readiness to ascribe to actual conditions the attributes of a 'perfect' market. (V:79)

Keynes admitted that the price level keeps in rough proportion
to the money supply, but he did not concede that the process can
be theoretically represented. His argument can be interpreted to
say that the price level is strictly indeterminate because the laws
of causation (*causa cognoscendi*) do not establish determinancy. A
scientific theory about the effect of money on prices was wrong
because it assumed, in accordance with the principle of indifference,
that if the money supply changes the incidental effects will cancel
each other out on average. Keynes replied that they did not
cancel out, but were of the essence, being a set of revised
positions between debtors and creditors, entrepreneurs and
wage-earners. The quantity theory of money was therefore based
on a false theory of causation, because it abstracted from change
at the atomic level, or from what he called 'subnormal
dispersion'. The whole point about inflation, the reason why it
was bad, was that subnormal dispersion did occur, meaning that
its effects did not cancel out.

The point that Keynes overlooked at the time is that the fluid
picture in Section II is inconsistent with the Ricardian interest
rate theory in Section III. The interest rate too is a price. If the
equilibrium level of prices is a myth, then so is the equilibrium
interest rate. Eventually, in the *General Theory*, Keynes reconciled
the themes of Sections II and III in the *Treatise on Money* by
expunging all Ricardian elements from his analysis, particularly
the natural rate of interest.

The Indeterminancy of Interest

In the *General Theory* Keynes took the further step after he had
identified the heart, the 'citadel', of classical theory, as the
natural rate of interest. There Keynes concluded that it was
Ricardian interest rate theory, rather than the Ricardian theory
of prices, that had always thwarted rational intuition and held
the army of insightful heretics at bay. The theory of interest in
the *General Theory* was meant to prove that interest rates are
logically indeterminate. He could then go on and show that
investment and output and employment are indeterminate as
well.

In the *General Theory* Keynes retracted his earlier belief that there is a natural rate of interest in the long run. The classical rules would apply in a hypothetical non-monetary economy, but in a real monetary economy the rate of interest cannot be determined by the intersection of the savings and investment schedules. Savings and investment alone are not in *pari materia*, and it is impossible to determine the interest rate at their point of intersection.

The propensity to save and the schedule of marginal efficiencies [of investment] are two curves which do not intersect anywhere, because they are not in *pari materia* and do not relate to the same variables. . . . There is no sense in which they can be said to intersect. (XIII:552)

Keynes shifted emphasis from the indeterminacy of prices to the indeterminacy of one special price, the rate of interest, because he connected indeterminacy and money. Whereas the *Treatise on Money* presents price indeterminacy—except for the rate of interest—as widespread in the economy, the *General Theory* focused only on the indeterminacy of the rate of interest. This is why the neo-Keynesians have regarded the *General Theory* not as the evolution of thought that Keynes said it was, but as a narrowing of focus and a special case.

R. F. Kahn and Joan Robinson had correctly understood that the *Treatise on Money* was supposed to be about economic indeterminacy, but in the *General Theory* 'technical monetary theory falls into the background' and there is no theory that relative prices are indeterminate. To the contrary, Keynes said that when there is full employment the classical theory comes into its own again, and he had 'no objection' to classical analysis.

If our central controls succeed in establishing an aggregate volume of output corresponding to full employment as nearly as is practicable, the classical theory comes into its own again from this point onwards. If we suppose the volume of output to be given, i.e. to be determined by forces outside the classical scheme of thought, then there is no objection to be raised against the classical analysis. (*GT*:378)

It was a significant reversal. He applied his previous theory of interest to prices, and his previous theory of prices to interest. Keynes described his intellectual passage from the *Treatise* to the *General Theory* as a 'natural evolution in a line of thought which . . . may strike the reader as a confusing change of view'. He located the outstanding fault in the earlier work in Sections III and IV, sections which the neo-Keynesians have followed; because those sections did not bring 'money into the economic scheme in an essential and peculiar manner', the *Treatise* 'showed a lack of emancipation from pre-conceived ideas' (*GT*:vi).

It is clear that the indeterminacy of the rate of interest displaced Keynes's earlier theory that prices in general are indeterminate. The *General Theory* not merely supplements the *Treatise on Money* but displaces it. The economy is not a complete flux after all, and it would operate according to physical laws except for the black hole of interest rate indeterminacy at its centre.

There is a simple means of reconciling Sections II and III in the *Treatise on Money*, which Keynes did not take, but which was taken by the neo-Keynesians. They kept the theory in Section III largely intact, with its Ricardian natural interest rate in the background and the newly understood significance of savings and investment in the foreground. However, they amended Keynes's theme in Section II from the philosophy of probability to the sociology of class and power, so that the economy was held to be indeterminate, not because of subnormal dispersion and the invalidity of the statistical principle of indifference, but because everything depended upon the struggle between capital and labour. Joan Robinson reconciled Section II with Section III by keeping III and reinterpreting II; she replaced animal spirits with ideology, and replaced the uncertainties of mortal knowledge with the uncertainties of the capitalist struggle.

One sign of the difference with Keynes is that the neo-Keynesians tend to think that there *is* an economic equilibrium, the problem being that capitalism does not get there. Joan Robinson writes of Keynes—and note that her 'normal rate of profit' is very analogous to the natural rate of interest except that there is no tendency towards it—as follows:

> He dealt only with forward-looking expectations of profits which would never be exactly fulfilled. All the same, he hankered after the concepts of a normal rate of profit and value of capital though he could not get them clear. (Robinson 1980a:80)[1]

She added that Keynes should have drawn on Ricardo! Had he done so he would have scuttled the *General Theory*, and of course it was Joan Robinson herself who hankered after Ricardian concepts. She thought economic indeterminancy was widespread throughout the whole economy, but that nevertheless behind it all was a conceivable equilibrium, a 'golden age'. Keynes came to locate economic indeterminancy in just one aspect of the economy, the rate of interest, but he had no concept of a reality behind the economy. Robinson was between Keynes's idea of the economy as no more than a cross-section of chaos, and the Ricardo–Marx idea of economics as a natural science.

The neo-Keynesians correctly stress the importance of uncertainty in Keynes's economics, but they change its meaning. Paul Davidson, for example, advocates a purer return to Keynes's own economics, and discusses uncertainty at length; yet he simply dismisses Chapter 12 in the *General Theory*, the uncertainty chapter, as 'analytically thin' (Davidson 1982:4). As Davidson points out, Keynes did say that this chapter was on a different level of abstraction from the rest of his book; however it is on a different level because it draws on Keynes's moral and probabilistic philosophies, not because it is superficial.

Another sign of the difference between Keynes and the neo-Keynesians is that neo-Keynesians do not associate money with uncertainty as Keynes did. 'Real forces emphasized, money assumed to accommodate' is how Davidson sums up neo-Keynesian economics (1972:31). For example, in Joan Robinson's *Accumulation of Capital*, the interest rate plays only a minor role,[2] while the indeterminancy of prices constitutes a major macro-economic problem. This then leads to policy differences; whereas Keynes emphasized the desirability of low rates of interest, neo-Keynesians tend to disregard interest rate controls in favour of more direct controls over prices and wages.

Finally, the political conclusion drawn is very different. If there is a general indeterminancy of all prices, then capitalism will be a fundamentally arbitrary system; whereas if only the interest rate is indeterminate, then only the overall level of investment would need to be regulated. Keynes concluded that there would be a need for macroeconomic policy but not for socialism. 'There is no more reason to socialize economic life than there was before. . . . It is in determining the volume, not the direction, of actual employment that the existing system has broken down' (*GT*:379).[3]

The Monetary Theory of Interest

Keynes traced the classical theory of interest back to Ricardo and J. S. Mill. That theory is that the amount saved depends positively upon the rate of interest; the amount invested depends negatively upon interest, which is the cost of borrowing; and at some equilibrium interest rate the supply of savings will equal the demand for savings, which is investment. As Keynes pointed out in the *Treatise on Money*, the picture is complicated by changes in hoarding and the money supply, which can both affect the amount of savings. The Ricardian method was to abstract from monetary changes and concentrate upon analysing the real economy underneath. For example, in one passage that is quoted in the *General Theory*, Ricardo explains that an expansion of the money supply ten or twenty times would not *permanently* affect the market rate of interest.

The interest of money is not regulated by the rate at which the Bank will lend, whether it be 5, 3 or 2 per cent, but by the rate of profit which can be made by the employment of capital, and which is totally independent of the quantity or of the value of money. Whether the Bank lent one million, ten millions, or a hundred millions, they would not permanently alter the market rate of interest. (Quoted in *GT*:190)

In other words, if transient monetary forces are forgotten, such as might arise from a hundredfold increase in money supply, there is a natural interest rate, at which the real forces in the economy—thrift and the productivity of capital—are co-ordinated. It was often recognized, of course, that in the actual world this natural rate of interest might never be exactly attained, but it remained a tendency, a point around which the capital markets would gravitate.

The consequences of this seemingly abstract picture are momentous, because if savings have an equilibrium tendency to be equal to investment, then it can be shown that the economy has a parallel equilibrium tendency towards full employment. The following proof is an abstract of a demonstration from J. S. Mill, whom Keynes singled out for criticism: total spending is investment plus consumption; total incomes are equal to savings plus consumption; therefore, by elementary arithmetic, if savings are equilibrated with investment, then in equilibrium total incomes equal total spending, which in turn means that the economy cannot have an equilibrium surplus of commodities (Mill, 1848:556–61). Expressing the conclusion otherwise, supply always creates its own demand, which is Say's Law, or otherwise, again, unemployment cannot be due to any fault in the economic system.

Keynes could have accepted the Ricardian interest theory in principle and simply declared his old position: that it took too long for the economy to reach equilibrium; that in the long run we are all dead. During the drafting of the *General Theory* he was strongly pressed towards this position by D. H. Robertson, and modern supporters of the classical theory still argue that Keynes simply failed to understand its logic and generality. He could also have argued plausibly that the classical theory had omitted some short-term variables, especially the influence of income levels upon savings, and so needed generalization. Once again, the effect would have been to show that the classical interest rate theory was not a plausible account of interest in the short run. This course was pressed upon Keynes by R. F. Harrod, but Keynes insisted that he had an entirely different theoretical structure to the classical system. 'Your mind is still in the classical world', he wrote back to Harrod. In correspondence with Harrod and Robertson, Keynes declared that it was not possible to reconcile his theory of interest with the classical theory, which had to be entirely abandoned. 'The classical theory of the rate of interest . . . makes no sense on any assumptions whatever' (XIII:557).

Against the classical theory that interest is determined in the market for savings and investment, Keynes proposed an equally simple and striking theory: that investment determines national income, and that the interest rate is determined by the supply and demand for money.

All that the propensity of the public towards hoarding can achieve is to determine the rate of interest at which the aggregate desire to hoard becomes equal to the available cash. The habit of overlooking the relation of the rate of interest to hoarding may be a part of the explanation why interest has been usually regarded as the reward of not-spending, whereas in fact it is the reward of not-hoarding. (*GT*:174)

Keynes returned to the theory, of medievals and mercantilists, that the rate of interest is a transient monetary phenomenon.

The Marginal Efficiency of Capital

If the rate of interest is determined by the demand and supply of money, then it cannot also be determined, as the classical economists said, by the demand and supply of savings. It is well known that Keynes argued that savings were influenced by income; but income could change, so the classics had left a variable out of their system. He also took a less known and more radical position, that there was no market for savings, and no way to bring savings and investment together in the market, because they are not commensurable. He wrote to Harrod:

If I had left out all the parts you object to about the classical school, you would simply have told me that you were largely in sympathy and liked it. But my attack on the classical school has brought to a head the fact that I have only half shifted you away from it.

My theory is essentially not a theory that the rate of interest is the factor which, allowing for changes in the level of income, brings the propensity to save into equilibrium with the inducement to invest. . . . It is the characteristic of these demand and supply schedules for savings that they have this unfortunate characteristic [of being indeterminate]. In truth there are no such things as these schedules. They are completely bogus. (XIII:548/551)

He found a technical error in the classical theory. Interest, according to the *General Theory*, 'has really no business to turn up at all in Marshall's *Principles of Economics*—it belongs to another branch of the subject' (*GT*:189). The monetary theory of interest was meant to replace the classical theory of interest because Keynes thought that the classical theory was mathematically *circular*. According to the classical theory, the rate of interest is determined by the demand and supply of savings, the demand for savings being intended investment. However, investment also depends upon the rate of interest in a different way, because the value of a return on investment is lower if it is in the far future, and how much so depends on the rate of interest. When Keynes was writing the *General Theory*, a mathematical expression which discounted future returns by the rate of interest had recently been devised by the American economist Irving Fisher, who referred to his expression as the rate of return on investment. Keynes, who developed a similar expression independently, called his the marginal efficiency of capital.

The return on investment was the sum, over time, of the expression $R(t)/(1 + r)^t$, where R was the return on investment in any time period t, r was the interest rate and the expression $(1 + r)^t$ discounted future returns at compound interest. Investment would be profitable if discounted returns, summed up over time, exceeded the cost of the investment.

According to the formula, the level of investment depends on the rate of interest; but according to the classical theory of interest, the interest rate itself is set by the equality of savings and investment. The classical theory was circular because interest determined investment and investment determined interest, and each one had to be known independently before the other one could be established. The significance of the formal definition of the marginal efficiency of capital was that the circularity could be brought out more clearly.

This conclusion serves to bring out even more the essential independence of the rate of interest as a factor in the economic situation, and the hopelessness in a non-stationary system of attempting to derive it, even in conditions of fullest monetary equilibrium, from the marginal efficiency of capital. For we have seen that, at best, the rate of interest tends to equality with the mean productive marginal efficiency of capital, and that the mean prospective marginal efficiency of capital depends on the . . . rate of interest. Thus unless we already know the prospective rate of interest, we cannot determine the prospective marginal efficiency of capital, and consequently we cannot discover the quantity towards equality with which the current rate of interest tends in conditions of fullest equilibrium. (XXIX:115)

As the above passage shows, Keynes did not argue that the classical theory was circular in a stationary economy with a known and fixed rate of interest. However, the theory became circular when it was applied to the real world, where the rate of interest could not be assumed in advance. 'The discovery of the marginal efficiency of capital looks very slight and scarcely more than formal,' Keynes wrote to Harrod, 'yet in my own progress of thought it was absolutely vital' (XIII:549). By this slight formula Keynes thought he had discovered a fallacy which, when pursued, showed that the invisible hand was not only invisible but meaningless as well. It meant that the interest rate was not determined in the market for loans.

Interest in an Indeterminate System

In the sense of the neo-classical writers, Keynes's theory of interest was a 'partial equilibrium' one, but in his own sense it expressed a much more general theory than theirs. Because he concentrated on money, they thought he was developing a short-run theory within a long-run classical framework. However, Keynes meant to develop an entirely new theory, which eschewed 'general equilibrium' and recognized that change is of the essence. His theory is meant as an account of an economy that is in flux because of uncertainty over the future. He believed that his theory was more general than the classical theory for the same reason that he believed that probability relations are more general than strict logical relations, because probability and change are of the world.

Keynes's new monetary theory of interest meant that interest was not determined primarily in the economic system, but by such external forces as conventions and psychological hopes and fears which were theoretically unpredictable in outcome. (A knowledge of both the general principles and the starting conditions would not be sufficient to predict the course of the interest rate.) The monetary theory of interest expressed the idea that the surface economy was always the only economy.

It might be more accurate, perhaps, to say that the rate of interest is a highly conventional, rather than a highly psychological, phenomenon. For its actual value is largely governed by the prevailing view as to what its value is expected to be. *Any* level of interest which is accepted with sufficient conviction as *likely* to be durable *will* be durable; subject, of course, in a changing society to fluctuations for all kinds of reasons round the expected normal. In particular, when M_1 is increasing faster than M, the rate of interest will rise, and *vice versa*. But it may fluctuate for decades about a level which is chronically too high for full employment. (*GT*:203)

The interest rate was indeterminate because of the general flux of economic affairs; the *General Theory* was general because it was the only way to impress a method of systematic thought upon the flux. But from the beginning, Keynes's intentions were misunderstood by his closest disciples.

Harrod understood indeterminancy as mathematical indeterminancy because he implicitly understood the economy as something translatable into a set of equations. In the mathematical sense, indeterminancy means that there are not enough equations for the classical theory to be able to solve for the interest rate, just as two straight lines in a cube may define a plane, but not a unique point of intersection. Keynes had said, as an important part of his attack on the classical theory of interest, that it forgot that savings depended upon income rather than on the interest rate, and that the classicals did not have an explanation for the level of national income. Harrod accepted this technical criticism of classical economics, but the appropriate response to mathematical indeterminancy is to introduce a third line into the cube, and so define a single point of intersection. Therefore Harrod defended the classical theory of interest as partly true. You say, he wrote to Keynes, that

Any method which endeavours to arrive at the rate of interest without bringing in liquidity preference is bound to be circular in the worst possible sense of the word. Yes, if income is variable. No, if income is constant. But, you say, income *is* variable. Granted. That brings us back to the old point:—they were wrong to take it as constant, but having made that mistake, their argument was quite logical. (XIII:554)

Keynes would not agree. His ultimate objection to the classical theory was not really that the classical account was mathematically indeterminate, but that it was only known *causa cognoscendi*, meaning that the interest rate is determined in a sequence of events that are too interrelated and complex for a scientific statement. If we stamp our feet, to vary an example from the *Treatise on Probability*, the bank rate may be shifted in its orbit, and economic science may never find the paths of causation. The classical theory is both logical, as Keynes admitted of Ricardo's theory (*GT*:192), and circular, which he said of Marshall's similar theory (*GT*:184), because it does not take account of objective chance, but abstracts from uncertainty and change. Classical theory assumes that the economic mechanism is bound by laws of regularity when in fact, Keynes believed, a monetary economy is bound only by a process of random change. This is the sense in which Keynes, in Section II of the *Treatise on Money*, regarded prices as indeterminate; and in the *General Theory* he applied the same approach to the theory of interest. Shortly after the above exchange with Harrod, Keynes tried unsuccessfully to convey this distinction to Hawtrey.

I agree that it would be more accurate to describe the classical theory as incomplete rather than as circular. But my point is that it is not incomplete in the sense that it deals with the special case rather than the general case. I maintain that as a theory it applies to no case at all. (XIII:593)

The classical theory is not incomplete because it deals with the special (partial equilibrium) case rather than the general (equilibrium) case, but it is incomplete in a different sense, in that it does not apply to the real world; 'it applies to no case at all', and can only be a tautology.

Value

Keynes's theory of value and monetary theory of interest were closely related, and in its initial drafts the *General Theory* criticized not the classical theory of interest, but the classical theory of value. In the preface to the *General Theory*, value was still said to be the main link between uncertainty and economic theory.

Our method of analysing the economic behaviour of the present under the influence of changing ideas about the future is one which depends on the interaction of supply and demand, and is in this way linked up with our fundamental theory of value. We are thus led to a more general theory, which includes the classical theory with which we are familiar, as a special case. (*GT*:Preface, vii)

Value was the link between tangible experience and the principles of probability, between the price of fish and the river of change. It is therefore indicative that Keynes's theories of value and interest are now remembered only through a mist. His labour theory of value is faintly represented in economic theory by the occasional measurement of economic quantities in terms of wage units, just as his theory of interest barely peers out from behind the *IS–LM* system that replaced it.

As might have been expected from Keynes's antipathy towards utilitarianism, he did not adopt a utilitarian theory of value, meaning that he did not say that value is price. He reverted to what he called a 'pre-classical' doctrine of value.

> I sympathize, therefore, with the pre-classical doctrine that everything is *produced by labour*, aided by what used to be called art and is now called technique, by natural resources which are free or cost a rent according to their scarcity or abundance, and by the results of past labour, embodied in assets, which also command a price according to their scarcity or abundance. It is preferable to regard labour, including, of course, the personal services of the entrepreneur and his assistants, as the sole factor of production, operating in a given environment of technique, natural resources, capital equipment and effective demand. This partly explains why we have been able to take the unit of labour as the sole physical unit which we require in our economic system, apart from units of money and of time. (*GT*:213)

Taken out of its context, this is a pre-classical theory of value only because Keynes says it is so. His theory of value seems the same as the Marxian theory of value, which perhaps explains why the neo-classical economists simply ignored it. The obvious point against saying that everything is produced by labour is that, under conditions of modern manufacture, capital can so thoroughly substitute for labour that it seems unrealistic to single labour out. To the contrary, with modern methods of production most things can probably be produced by capital alone.

Neo-Keynesians and other followers of Ricardo can reply that the capital had to be produced by labour as well as capital, and can trace back the processes of production to the original labour; but such long-run retrospectivity is not Keynes's theory, and is against the spirit of his analysis. Nevertheless, Keynes's theory of value should be taken seriously, as he took it seriously. The comment that Joan Robinson broadcast, that Keynes never spent the twenty minutes necessary to understand the [Ricardian] theory of value,[4] was part of her general complaint that he failed to see the Ricardian structure hidden beneath the economic surface; but Keynes did not accept that there was a hidden economic reality.

To understand what Keynes did mean by pre-classical economics, it is instructive to look at his own source. Today we take our idea of classical economics from Keynes. A classical economist believes that the economy is self-regulating because savings and investment are brought into equilibrium in the capital market, and he believes in Say's Law, that supply creates its own demand, so that a permanent surplus of commodities and sustained unemployment are impossible. However, the original definition was cast in different terms. Keynes took the term classical economics from Marx:

'The classical economists' was a name invented by Marx to cover Ricardo and James Mill and their *predecessors*, that is to say for the founders of the theory which culminated in Ricardian economics. I have become accustomed, perhaps perpetrating a solecism, to include in 'the classical school' the *followers* of Ricardo . . . (*GT*:3)

And Marx defined classical economics not in terms of Say's Law or full employment, but in terms of value. This is the definition of classical economics in *Capital*, which Keynes presumably drew upon:

As regards value in general, it is the weak point of the classical school of Political Economy that it nowhere, expressly and with full consciousness, distinguishes between labour, as it appears in the value of a product, and the same labour, as it appears in the use-value of that product. Of course the distinction is practically made. But it has not the least idea, that when the difference between various kinds of labour is treated as purely quantitative, their qualitative unity or equality, and therefore their reduction to abstract human labour, is implied. . . .

Once for all I may here state, that by classical Political Economy, I understand that economy which, since the time of W. Petty, has investigated the real relations of production in bourgeois society, in contradistinction to vulgar economy, which deals with appearances only, ruminates without ceasing on the materials long since provided by scientific economy, and there seeks plausible explanations of the most obtrusive phenomena, for bourgeois daily use . . . (Marx 1954, i (4):81).

Elsewhere Marx says that classical economics, as distinguished from vulgar economics, 'seeks to grasp the inner connection in contrast to the multiplicity of outward forms' (Marx 1971:500). Marx understood classical economics in a way that in many respects came down to the usual interpretation, but was cast in terms of abstract labour in value.

Classical economics is literally the economics which, by assuming a unique standard of value, can demonstrate the

superior reality of a hidden economy. It was a term of
disparagement from Keynes, but it was partly a term of praise
from Marx, who also believed in a superior hidden economy. The
Marxian objection to the classical school was that it did not
follow its own value theory through consistently enough, but
nevertheless Marx praised Ricardo as the first scientific economist.

By comparison with the 'pre-classics', Marx assumed that all
labour could be reduced to homogeneous labour *power* even
though it might vary in productivity. The classical theory of
value, he said, properly meant that 'all labour is equal human
labour, and consequently labour of equal quality' (Marx 1954, I,
i (3.3)). According to Marx, the Ricardian contribution was not
to make value depend upon labour, which even the 'vulgar'
economists then did, but to assume this qualitative homogeneity
of labour, which the vulgar economists did not. Marx's criticism
of Ricardo was that his assumption of qualitative homogeneity of
labour power was not enunciated 'expressly and with full
consciousness', even though in practice Ricardo had assumed a
unique standard of value.

The significance of assuming a unique standard of value is that
scientific economics requires that commodities be brought into
pari materia with each other on some genuine basis,[5] if the
economist is not to be overwhelmed with detail. The classical
labour theory of value stood for economic science, which was
brought out when Marx defended his theory against Aristotle. In
his *Ethics* Aristotle had said that relative prices are indeterminate
in principle, because there is no genuine commensurability
between unlike things. To use Aristotle's example, the exchange
ratios between beds, houses and money do not reflect any
underlying reality, but are a 'makeshift for practical purposes',
signifying nothing. I have italicized the essential point below.

What money does for us is to act as a guarantee of exchange in the
future. . . . So money acts as a measure which, by making things
commensurable, enables us to equate them. Without exchange there
would be no association, without equality there would be no exchange,
without commensurability there would be no equality. Strictly speaking,
things so widely different cannot become commensurable; but in relation to
demand a sufficient degree of accuracy is possible. (Aristotle, *Ethics*:
1133 619)

This belief that the economy is indeterminate characterizes

pre-classical economics in general. Marx's reply against Aristotle was that labour power does provide the essential element of commensurability between commodities, because labour is qualitatively the same in all respects. His Ricardian foundation was not the labour theory of value, but *commensurability*, or being able to put commodities on an underlying basis, the precondition for an abstract science of economics.[6]

Ricardo was the first scientific economist because he assumed an invariant standard of value, whereas the medieval labour theory of value had quite a different meaning. Value referred to the intrinsic, non-economic worth of things; labour might be the real factor of production because it is an image of the divine work, which is *ex nihilo*, without material aids. It is only the poet who produces the poem, although he is helped by his spectacles and pen. In this sense labour could not be used as a standard unit, and in fact the pre-classics regarded scientific economics as impossible.

When he was writing the *General Theory*, Keynes announced in a letter to George Bernard Shaw that the 'Ricardian foundations of Marxism would be knocked away'. Today the Ricardian foundations of Marxism are regarded as the labour theory of value; but since Keynes also had a labour theory of value, this is not what he meant, and neither is it how Marx understood his Ricardian foundations. Keynes meant to show that there is no such thing as the hidden economy, that the economy of appearances is the only one, and that the Ricardian method 'of adopting a hypothetical world remote from experience as though it were the world of experience and then living in it consistently' was to be condemned for its abstractedness rather than praised for its science.

In the same sense, he also knocked away the Ricardian foundations of neo-classical economics. A non-monetary economy would have underlying rules, but commensurability could not apply in a monetary economy. By unconsciously assuming it, Keynes's own teacher Alfred Marshall had been led to deal with monetary problems in a non-monetary context.

Marshall expressly states that he is dealing with *relative* exchange values. The proposition that the prices of a ton of lead and a ton of tin are 15 pounds and 90 pounds means no more to him in this context than that the value of a ton of tin in terms of lead is six tons. . . .

Now the conditions required for the 'neutrality' of money, in the sense in which this is assumed in—again to take this book as a leading example—Marshall's *Principles of Economics*, are, I suspect, precisely the same as those which will insure that crises *do not occur*. (XIII:409–10)

After saying that it was a mere matter of convenience to assume a uniform standard of purchasing power, to add tin to lead, Marshall had gone on, as Keynes noted, to compare the economy to the solar system (Marshall 1920, iii:51–2). The convenience of economists was like that of astronomers who assume a 'mean sun', whereas the actual sun passes the meridian sometimes before and sometimes after noon by the clock. Marshall thought that because he could add tin and lead together he could also assume that the economy was like a barter economy, without the disturbances caused by money.[7]

In the *General Theory* Keynes attacked again. It was a grave objection to the Marshallian concept of national income that 'The community's output of goods and services is a non-homogeneous complex which cannot be measured, strictly speaking, except in certain special cases, as for example when all the items of one output are included in the same proportions in another output' (*GT*:38). This famous passage does not mean that Keynes was challenging index numbers,[8] but he was refuting Marshall and Pigou, who were 'covertly introducing changes in *value*' in their economic theories. Keynes conceded, in this section of the *General Theory*, that it was useful to refer to the national income and other statistical constructs, for convenience, when nothing rested on the particular form of measurement. However, Marshall was invalidly drawing on an assumption of convenience to 'erect a quantitative science' of economics. The answer is that we cannot rely in theory upon what we may assume for simplicity in practice. We may speak of the national income and the price level, applying 'some broad element of judgement' rather than strict calculation, but we cannot thereby deduce a normal theory of value or the commensurability of 'incommensurable collections of miscellaneous objects'. We cannot draw on the principle of indifference to cancel out the atomic variability in the economy. Classical economics had abstracted from variability to erect a natural science of economics, when what was required was a system based on the fact of complexity itself.

The theory of value expressed Keynes's general method and

justified his theory of interest. In particular, the theory of value, which is in Chapter 16 of the *General Theory*, showed that there could be no natural rate of interest. It therefore cleared the way for Keynes's alternative theory, in Chapter 17, that we must think in terms of a complex set of interest rates.

It is much preferable to speak of capital as having a yield over the course of its life in excess of its original cost, than as being *productive*. For the only reason why an asset offers a prospect of yielding during its life services having an aggregate value greater than its initial supply price is because it is *scarce*; and it is kept scarce because of the competition of the rate of interest on money. If capital becomes less scarce, the excess yield will diminish, without its having become less productive—at least in the physical sense. (*GT*:213)

There is no natural rate of interest, because it follows from the theory of value that the productivity of capital is only an accounting figure. The pre-classical theory of value, signature of the age-long tradition of common-sense economics, took complexity at its face value. It meant that there is no long-run equilibrium (nor a Marxian dialectic propelled by hidden contradictions in the economy), but that the seething mind-boggling mass of surface fact is all there really is, that economics is in the realm of the ephemeral. The economics of Ricardo and Marx and Marshall, arch determinists who dreamed of economic science, were to be supplanted in the West by the economics of transition and meaningless change.

Keynes's theories of value and interest represent his attempt to formalize a new and non-deterministic method of economics. Perhaps there are other ways to do the same, but so far this has been the only one. The economists heard his song, but when they dissected the words they concluded that these theories could only be the result of some most elementary ignorance on his part. This was rare unanimity; but now they had to express Keynes's non-deterministic theory in terms of their own.

Notes to Chapter 7

1. See also *The Generalization of the General Theory*: 'Real forces have a roundabout influence on the actual rate of interest. . . . Keynes' theory [which] treated the rate of interest as determined by the

demand and supply of money . . . was a useful simplification in the
pioneering days of the theory' (Robinson 1979:139).

As these and other statements show, Joan Robinson did not
dispute the classical doctrine that there is a point of economic
balance and equilibrium, with a natural rate of interest. She also
believed that Keynes was unrealistic to think that interest rates could
be held down by monetary measures. What she objected to was the
neo-classical assumption that the capitalist economy had any *tendency*
towards equilibrium. Joan Robinson conceded that there is equilibrium, but because capitalism is a power system it cannot be
realized. Her position and Keynes's may seem similar, and Joan
Robinson slurred over the difference, but they signify approaches to
the economy that are a world apart.

2. The interest rate is not brought into the formal analysis until
   Chapter 24 of the *Accumulation of Capital*.
3. Of course it is possible to combine elements from Keynes and the
   neo-Keynesians. See for example M. Milgate (1982), who super-
   imposes a long-run Ricardian theory on Keynes's belief that
   monetary forces are fundamental.
4. The significance of this canard is the greater because it has been
   seized upon by neo-classical economists as a reason for them also to
   disregard Keynes's theory of value (see for example Leijonhufvud
   1968:33). Joan Robinson was quoting Gerald Shove at a time when
   he was immersed in Ricardian economics. She was hostile to neo-
   classical value theory, which she declared to be an elaboration of the
   theory of index numbers, by implication not worth twenty minutes'
   deliberation. She was accusing Keynes of being indifferent not to
   neo-classical, but to Ricardian, value theory.

   The only economist who took Keynes's theory of value seriously
   was Hugh Townshend, who seems to have enjoyed an intellectual
   empathy with Keynes after the *General Theory*. Townshend said that
   the culmination of the *General Theory* was 'a self consistent new theory
   of value, subsuming the new theory of interest at which he [Keynes]
   had originally been aiming' (*Economic Journal*, 1937). As a matter of
   pure theory, Victoria Chick has argued that Keynes's use of the wage
   unit for the measurement of economic quantities 'distinguishes
   Keynes' analysis sharply from neo-classical theories' (see Chick
   1985).

   I would add that there is a distinction to be made between
   Keynes's use of wage units for index number measurement and his
   theory of value, even though the latter was a reason for the former.
   The selection of wage units was partly an arbitrary choice in the face
   of the index number problem. Keynes's theory of value was not

arbitrary, as is clear from the preface to the *General Theory*, but fundamental. Marx accused Ricardo of vitiating his analysis by failing to differentiate between value as an index number and value as a generator of concepts; and Malthus was guilty of the same confusion. Keynes made the distinction, see for example XXIX:73: 'These partly insoluble difficulties of quantitative description do not arise in our causal analysis, which is *strictly logical* in itself and is subject, in practice not to essentially insoluble difficulties, but only to the actual imperfections of our knowledge.'

5. Contrary to what Keynes says ('classical economics was a name invented by Marx to cover Ricardo and James Mill'), Marx did *not* call James Mill, whom he detested, a classical economist. However, Keynes's error is suggestive, because Marx did attribute to Mill the idea that all commodities can be aggregated into one commodity, and he bracketed Mill with the Ricardians in this one respect (Marx 1954, I, iii (1C)).

6. The point is not that Keynes was familiar with Aristotle's economics, or that Marx interpreted Aristotle correctly, but that Keynes understood classical economics in much the same way as Marx. However, Keynes did study Aristotle's *Ethics* when he was formulating his own early philosophy; and shortly before writing the *General Theory* Keynes defended, in an essay on ancient currencies, Aristotle's pronouncements concerning monetary units of exchange.

The pre-classical theories of money and value both derive from Aristotle, who declared interest to be a return on *money*, which he said was barren. The medieval arguments against usury go back to him. In addition, although Aristotle did not formulate a labour theory of value, the labour theory developed by Magnus Albertus and Thomas Aquinas is usually said to be in the Aristotelian tradition. More modern descendants of the same tradition include John Locke, who adopted the pre-classical theories of both interest and value, and Thomas Malthus, who as Keynes said was educated in the 'Cambridge of [William] Paley', meaning medieval ethics.

Aristotle and the scholastics did not consider that there could be a determinate economic system, because they regarded economic motives as sub-rational. The passage quoted from Aristotle occurs after a discussion of justice; Aristotle believed that there were absolute principles of justice (even though in political practice different rules applied). However, the market cannot offer justice, because there are no absolute economic principles. The moderns turn this way of thinking upside down—there are underlying economic principles, but justice has only an arbitrary meaning. This inversion has been analysed by Hannah Arendt, who distinguished sharply between the pre-classical and classical theories of value, and suggested that the latter was an attempt to re-establish standards in a world which had lost its absolute ideals (see Arendt 1958:163–6).

7. In Appendix I of the *Principles* Marshall gave a—very wrong— utilitarian account of Ricardo and his theory of value, and then concluded by defending Ricardo against nameless critics, who, he said, 'attempt to disprove doctrines as to the ultimate tendencies, the causes of causes, the *causae causantes*, of the relations between cost of production and value, by means of arguments based on the causes of temporary changes, and short-period fluctuations of value. Doubtless nearly everything they say when expressing their own opinions is true in the sense in which they mean it; some of it is new and much of it is improved in form. But they do not appear to make any progress towards establishing their claim to have discovered a new doctrine of value which is in sharp contrast to the old; or which calls for any considerable demolition, as distinguished from development and extension of the old doctrine.'

   In such a manner, Thomas Malthus's argument, that there is no such thing as an invariant standard of value, was dismissed without being named. The invariant labour standard of value became the invariant utility standard, and the concept of ultimate economic tendencies, *causae causantes*, was reaffirmed.

8. Don Patinkin has dismissed this passage by saying that Keynes was unaware there is a simple index number method—national accounting—which could have resolved his reservations about the homogeneity of commodities (see Patinkin 1982:129). Keynes did know of this 'solution', as study of the *General Theory* (p. 38 *et seq.*) shows, but since his early paper on index numbers he had disputed its validity.

   Patinkin's misunderstanding is not peculiar to neo-classical economists. For example, the Marxist Maurice Dobb wrote concerning the classical debate over the existence of a unique standard of value: 'To a modern this search for an . . . invariable standard [of value] is apt to appear curious and even meaningless: so much so that it is sometimes dismissed as a phantom or else just the familiar 'index number problem' in an old fashioned guise' (Dobb 1973:184)

   Marx was the last writer, before Keynes, to have treated pre-classical monetary and value theory as aspects of the more general philosophy from which they were derived.

8

The Vision Translated

The crisis [in macroeconomics] results from the problem
that Keynesian macroeconomics has never been anchored
in the normal paradigm of theoretical economics. . . . That
is one side of a crisis that has been smouldering for many
years. On the other side the [neo-classical] paradigm . . .
fails to explain facts that everybody can see.

J. Tobin, in A. Klamer, *The New Classical Macroeconomics*

Between Keynes and the Keynesians who inherited his theories
there lay a wide divide. His philosophy they did not dream of;
their philosophy he knew and rejected. Yet the Keynesians had
to bridge the divide, and to translate his ideas into their
mechanics. The practical consequence was the Keynesian period
from about 1945 to 1970, which, to judge by its results only, has
probably been the most successful of all, with low unemployment,
low inflation and reasonable growth. Yet, cut off from Keynes's
vision, Keynesian economic theory was inconsistent and
intellectually indefensible.

Keynes's theory was soon replaced by Keynesianism, and
Keynesianism was in turn replaced by neo-classical economics,
which regarded Keynes's theory as a useful but inaccurate
snapshot of an economy that was best portrayed by differential
equations. But neo-classical theory, which praised the usefulness
of Keynes's theories and yet contested their validity, was itself
between two poles of thought. Monetarism went to the other pole
when it drew its formal theory from classical economists, without
paying obeisance to Keynes. There has been a tendency to move
away from the economics of Keynes, but because of the growing
disillusionment with monetarism there has also been a new
interest in his method. However, this new interest in Keynes will
be unproductive unless it is recognized that he departed from

conventional thought at an epistemological point outside economics. 'Post Keynesianism', wrote Robert Solow (1979:344), 'seems to be more a state of mind than a theory.' That indeed was how Keynes understood it, and 'our minds have not yet met' was one of his phrases, although by a state of mind Solow meant a state of prejudice or partiality, which is not what Keynes meant.

Ricardo had understood economics as the science of equilibrium. After Keynes, the neo-classical economists came to understand it as the mechanics of a transitional path to equilibrium, but they still had a notion of an economy being definable by a set of equations. In Keynes's economics there is no general mathematical theory because neither the variables nor the parameters behind the equations can be comprehensively defined. 'As soon as one is dealing with the influence of expectations and of transitory experience,' he wrote immediately after the *General Theory*, 'one is, in the nature of things, outside the realm of the formally exact' (XIV:2).

Since the difference between Keynes and the Keynesians has already been analysed in two challenging books by Paul Davidson (1972, 1982), I will briefly indicate where I depart from him. Davidson targets the conventional Keynesians, because they combine Keynes's economics with classical economics. I argue that *none* of Keynes's followers, not even Davidson, have adopted Keynes's theory of probability or his moral economic science. I agree that the conventional Keynesians misunderstood Keynes because they saw him through classical eyes, but the neo-Keynesians also distorted Keynes, because to really follow Keynes's theory of uncertainty they would have to abandon Ricardo and Marx. Both the neo-Keynesian socialists and the conventional Keynesians are separated from Keynes by the same chasm, which is deeper than Davidson acknowledges, of Keynes's method, which comes from his idealism. Therefore, unlike Davidson, I am not directly interested in the particular assumptions made by the conventional Keynesians, and my main theme is not their defects but Keynes's own method.

Hume and Ricardo

The idea of economics as a moral science originated not with Keynes, but (probably) with the person whom he regarded as a paragon among economists, Thomas Malthus. 'If only Malthus, instead of Ricardo, had been the parent from which nineteenth-century economics proceeded, what a much wiser and richer place the world would be today' (X:101). Malthus, personal friend and intellectual antagonist of Ricardo, spent the first part of his adult life contending that there was a tendency for an excess supply of population, and the second arguing that there was a tendency for the demand to be inadequate to employ the population. Although he is best known for the first part, being the author of the *Essay on Population* which inspired the evolutionary theories of Charles Darwin, Keynes described Malthus's second theory, concerning inadequate demand, as more far-reaching. For in order to establish that demand could be systematically inadequate, Malthus developed a new idea of economic science. Malthus, as Marx put it, sinned against science.

'The science of political economy', Malthus wrote in the preface to his *Principles*, 'bears a nearer relation to the science of morals and politics than to that of mathematics.' It does not matter that Ricardo, who was the person being accused here of mathematical economics, never wrote an equation. The real question was the degree of *abstractedness* that is appropriate to economics. Keynes understood the methodological issue in Malthus's terms almost exactly:

According to Malthus's good common-sense notion prices and profits are primarily determined by something which he described, though none too clearly, as 'effective demand'. Ricardo favoured a much more rigid approach [than Malthus's effective demand], went behind 'effective demand' to the underlying conditions of money . . . and looked on Malthus's method as very superficial. But Ricardo, in the course of simplifying the many successive stages of his highly abstract argument, departed, necessarily and more than he himself was aware, away from the actual facts; whereas Malthus, by taking up the tale much nearer its conclusion, had a firmer hold on what may be expected to happen in the real world. . . . When one has painfully escaped from the intellectual domination of these [Ricardian] pseudo-arithmetical doctrines, one is able, perhaps for the first time for a hundred years, to comprehend the real significance of the vaguer intuitions of Malthus. (X:88)

Malthus's moral science of economics closely resembles the principles of Burke's doctrine of expediency in politics, and his criticisms of Ricardo recall Burke's criticisms of the arbitrary abstractions of the liberals. In essence, Malthus put principle and pragmatism ahead of scientific abstraction; Keynes said that Malthus's approach to economics was through the 'best of all routes', namely, through moral and political philosophy.

The moral science was cast more in negative than in positive terms. 'Certain eminent persons', Malthus said, 'fear of destroying the simplicity of a general rule' and 'overlook any circumstances that may interfere with the generality of the principle' (Malthus 1951 edn.:12). He held that the principles of political economy are cast at the wrong level to be truly general and invariant; that there is no general theory of political economy; and that theories, being only partial, must be interpreted according to the changing circumstances, rather than the circumstances abstracted from according to the theory; and he implied that the choice between these theories required a knowledge that was not to be found within political economy. The Ricardian method, he held, overlooked the problem of unemployment and deficient demand in the economy because it violated these principles, which were the principles of pragmatism.

Malthus focused, as much as did Keynes, on the surface phenomena of economic life, and looked for no deeper meanings in economic abstraction. Although like Keynes he recognized the need for formal structures of economic thought, he too stressed the dangers of long chains of economic logic.

I certainly am disposed to refer frequently to things as they are, as the only way of making one's writings practically useful to society, and I think also the only way of being secure from falling into the errors of the taylors of Laputa, and by a slight mistake at the outset arrive at conclusions the most distant from the truth. (Malthus to Ricardo, quoted in X:97)

Keynes made similar criticisms of Ricardo, but the closest parallel was Keynes's complaint that the classical economics of von Hayek was 'an extraordinary example of how, starting with a mistake, a remorseless logician can end up in Bedlam' (XIII: 252).

Ricardo identified economic science and economic equilibrium. Ricardo is often said to have been the first scientific economist; he was also the first to analyse the economy as though it were in permanent equilibrium. Prices were held by him to be proportional to the money supply, and there was a natural rate of interest, dependent only on real forces and not on financial conditions. When Ricardo said that changes in the money supply 'would not permanently alter the rate of interest', the word 'permanently' meant 'according to the theory'. For as Keynes noted, Ricardo believed that the surface of economic life was sub-rational and outside the proper scope of economic science.

For Ricardo expressly repudiated any interest in the *amount* of the national dividend, as distinct from its distribution. In this he was assessing correctly the character of his own theory. But his successors, less clear-sighted, have used the classical theory in discussions concerning the causes of wealth. *Vide* Ricardo's letter to Malthus of October 9, 1820: 'Political Economy you think is an enquiry into the nature and causes of wealth—I think it should be called an enquiry into the laws which determine the division of the produce of industry amongst the classes who concur in its formation. No law can be laid down respecting quantity, but a tolerably correct one can be laid down respecting proportions. Every day I am more satisfied that the former enquiry is vain and delusive, and the latter only the true objects of the science.' (*GT*:4)

Ricardo's belief that economic science required economic equilibrium led him to criticize the older classical economic theory, which had accounted for both equilibrium and the path to it, the theory that Keynes himself held in the Tract. In this theory, *eventually* prices would be proportional to the money supply, and *eventually* the interest rate would disengage from monetary influences and reach its natural level. In the meantime, although there is change, there are the reference points of equilibrium, beacons in the river of change, which are all that a science of economics requires. This theory was not only older than the Ricardian, but it had impeccable scientific credentials, because its author was the person whom Keynes regarded as the first classical economist of all—David Hume, philosopher, now in his manifestation of political economist:

Hume a little later [after Locke] had a foot and a half in the classical world. For Hume began the practice among economists of stressing the importance of the equilibrium position as compared with the ever-shifting transition towards it, though he was still enough of a mercantilist not to overlook the fact that it is in the transition that we actually have our being. (*GT*:343)

Although Hume believed that money had 'chiefly a fictitious value', he also acknowledged, which Ricardo did not, that a decrease in its amount would lead to a temporary deficiency of demand. 'There is always an interval before manners be adjusted to their new situation; and this interval is pernicious to industry when gold and silver are diminishing' (Hume 1955:40). In this, Hume may have been true to his own method, for as Keynes once stressed, in the *Treatise on Probability*, Hume was not deceived by the superficialities of mathematicians into thinking that the law of large numbers can solve the problems of causation. But Ricardo held it to be an 'erroneous view of Mr Hume' that money can call forth goods (Sraffa 1951–73, V:524), and Alfred Marshall and his disciples followed the Ricardian assumption of permanent equilibrium.

Classical economics was therefore a two-headed beast, with a Ricardian version that assumed permanent equilibrium and Hume's method, which assumed only an eventual equilibrium. Keynes especially objected to the particular assumption of the Ricardian system, its tendency to assume away the transition. However, he also objected in a more general way to both versions of classical economics.

Mathematical Economics

'Human society, when we contemplate it in a certain abstract and philosophical light, appears as a great, an immense machine, whose regular and harmonious movements produce a thousand agreeable effects'. So wrote Adam Smith (1759:316), and economists still tend to think of the economy as being like a machine. There is a set of levers, such as government policy, expectations, etc., called the independent variables; and a set of outputs, such as prices, called the dependent variables. A theory of the economy is understood to mean writing down the

blueprints of the machine, which may be why a theory is referred
to as a 'model' of the economy. The same metaphor applies to
neo-Keynesian economics, although it is not quantitative, and
we cannot clearly read the dials on the machine.

When Keynes said that economics was not a natural science,
he meant partly that the economy could not be specified as a
comprehensive blueprint, because the mechanical metaphor does
not apply. 'The object of our analysis is, not to provide a
machine, or method of blind manipulation, which will furnish an
infallible answer, but to provide ourselves with an organized and
orderly method of thinking out particular problems. . . . This is
the nature of economic thinking' (GT:297). By this 'method of
thinking' Keynes meant not inferential thinking, but probabilistic
thinking, where strict inference does not always work. Although
Keynes's opposition to mathematical economics, or more strictly
to abstract economics, has been painted as idiosyncratic, it was
part of a well defined philosophy, which is particularly crucial to
understanding the *General Theory*.

In the first place, because Keynes regarded the economy as an
unbounded and yet interrelated swirl of events, he did not think
that it was meaningful to distinguish between the dependent and
independent variables of the system, between the output and the
levers. There are *no* truly independent variables, because
everything influences everything else, and no matter how general
the economic theory it cannot pick up all the interactions. In
theory, we make the division between dependent and independent
variables, but it is only a mental division. 'The division of the
determinants of the economic system into the two groups of given
factors and independent variables is, of course, quite arbitrary
from any absolute standpoint. The division must be made
entirely on the basis of experience . . .' (*GT*:247). Therefore he
held that it was not possible to isolate the effects of changing one
of the variables of an economic system, because the supposedly
independent variables were all interrelated, although in different
ways at different times.

Second, according to Keynes, economics cannot deal with the
real workings of the economy, because it does not deal with the
real atomic causal units, which are judgements of value and
phantasmagoric fears and desires that are unquantifiable. In his
essay on Edgeworth, Keynes says that 'the atomic hypothesis

which has worked so splendidly in Physics breaks down in Psychics', meaning in mathematical economics; and in the *General Theory* he warns that the independent variables of the theory are only aggregations, and that 'these again would be capable of being subjected to further analysis, and are not, so to speak, our ultimate atomic independent elements' (*GT*:247).

Rather than dealing with *causa essendi*, or *causae verae*, as Keynes also called them, economics can deal only with categories that are consolidated beyond the point where true causation can apply. The variables of economic theory are 'fallible indexes, dubious approximations at that, with much doubt added as to what, if anything, they are indexes or approximations of' (X:262). The economic machine which the economists typically have in mind is never the real machine, the workings of which cannot be represented, because economics is always expressed in the wrong terms for true causation.

Finally, the unboundedness of economic theory and the impossibility of true causation make the economy so complex that *in principle* it is not representable by mathematics. Because economic categories are only approximate and analogical, while the influences upon them are complex and unbounded, mathematical reasoning cannot apply. Given these insubstantial relationships and fluid categories, the best that mathematical economics can do is to illustrate the complexities of the economy by demonstrating its own limits.

It is, I think, of the essential nature of economic exposition that it gives, not a complete statement, which even if it were possible, would be prolix and complicated to the point of obscurity but a sample statement, so to speak, out of all the things which could be said. (XIII:470)

I do not myself attach much value to [mathematical] manipulations of this kind; and I would repeat the warning . . . that they involve just as much tacit assumption as to what variables are taken as independent (partial differentials being ignored throughout) as does ordinary discourse, whilst I doubt if they carry us any further than ordinary discourse can. Perhaps the best purpose served by writing them down is to exhibit the extreme complexity of the relationship between prices and the quantity of money, when we attempt to express it in a formal manner. (*GT*:305)

Probably this is why Keynes declared it important that a

theory should not be quantified, because a quantified theory 'loses its generality and its value as a mode of thought'. To quantify a theory is to tear the theory from its context, when what is important is the relation between the theory and the context. 'Progress in economics consists almost entirely in a progressive improvement in the choice of models', which is to say progress occurs through new and more revealing orderings of the swirl of economic data. The role of economic theory was to present to the intuition material that had been organized for assimilation. Keynes believed economic theory should be 'lean', its role being to convey only a general insight. He had the opposite to the usual positivist idea, which represents intuition as the handmaid of science, mainly providing hypotheses for testing. In his philosophy, intuition is paramount over science as a criterion of truth.

Hence the extreme complexity of the actual course of events. Nevertheless, these seem to be the factors which it is useful and convenient to isolate. If we examine any actual problem along the lines of the above schematism, we shall find it more manageable; and our practical intuition (which can take account of a more detailed complex of facts than can be treated on general principles) will be offered a less intractable material upon which to work. (*GT*:249)

Similarly, Keynes did not conceive of economics as a giant theory unified in all of its aspects, with economic galaxies built out of the economic atoms. If economics is not a natural science, based on real atomic units, it cannot be unified. 'Between two different ideas we would examine,' said Locke, 'we cannot always find such mediums as we can connect one to another in all parts of the deduction' (Locke 1690, Bk. 4, iii (4)). Keynes's macroeconomics seemingly drew its assumptions out of thin air, or at least without reference to any micro theory, because it was based on a probabilistic logic.

Keynes accepted that there were two entirely different theories of economics, one at the micro level in terms of demand and supply, and another at the macro level involving money. He did not try to reconcile the two accounts, his only conclusion being that it was necessary to have a *correct* subdivision of economics.

We have all of us become used to finding ourselves sometimes on the one side of the moon and sometimes on the other, without knowing what

route or journey connects them, related, apparently, after the fashion of
our waking and our dreaming lives. . . . The right dichotomy is, I
suggest, between the Theory of the Individual Industry or Firm and of
the rewards and the distribution between different uses of a *given*
quantity of resources on the one hand, and the Theory of Output and
Employment *as a whole* on the other hand. (*GT*:292–3)

The obvious objection to Keynes's philosophy of action is that
there will be different intuitions held by different people, so that
relying on intuition means that the advance of knowledge will be
halted. Keynes certainly did not agree that progress would be
halted, but if we recall the *Treatise on Probability*, we do not have
any choice. We draw upon intuition not only for our hypotheses,
but also to interpret the tests and very meanings of theories,
because exactitude is beyond us. If this means that we must for
ever live in a twilight of probability, then, to transpose the theme
in the *Treatise on Probability*, it is best to recognize our limitations
and act upon them instead of representing to ourselves that our
methods of knowledge are more powerful than they actually are.

Keynes's opposition to mathematical economics, or more
strictly to long chains of abstract reasoning, should not be
dismissed as a character quirk or a peevish reaction to his own
failure to develop a mathematical theory of economics. His
opposition long pre-dates his interest in formal economic theory.
He satirized mathematical economics a decade before the *General
Theory* in his early essays on Marshall and Edgeworth, the latter
of whom he regarded as the leading mathematical economist and
econometrician of his day:

All his intellectual life through he felt his foundations slipping away
from under him. . . . Edgeworth knew that he was skating on thin ice;
and as life went on his love of skating and his distrust of the ice
increased, by a malicious fate, *pari passu*. He is like one who seeks to
avert the evil eye by looking sideways, to escape the censure of fate by
euphemism, calling the treacherous sea Euxine and the unfriendly
guardians of truth the kindly ones.[1] (X:262)

We can trace Keynes's opposition to mathematics in the social
sciences generally back to the *Treatise on Probability*, where he
expressed his preference for systems of words rather than
symbols, because words contain a power of metaphorical
suggestion. 'I . . . have not the same lively hope as Concordet, or

even as Edgeworth, "éclairer les Sciences morales et politiques par le flambeau de l'Algèbre".' Going back even further, mathematics presumably would not apply in an organic unity, where the secondary 'reflex values' would make any analysis intolerably difficult. Right or wrong, Keynes's opposition to mathematical economics was part of a consistent philosophy which attempted to bring formal thought to bear on probabilistic experience.[2]

A common criticism is that Keynes followed Alfred Marshall's method of partial equilibrium economics, instead of general equilibrium—meaning that Keynes theorized about a subsection of the economic machine, whereas modern general equilibrium economics examines the whole machine with all of its feedback loops. However, this division between partial and general again assumes that the economy is a machine rather than an organic unity, and Keynes did not think himself that he had the same method as Marshall. Keynes approved of Marshall's saying that economics can be understood as a set of principles, rather than as a set of theories:

'Ricardo and his chief followers did not make clear to others, it was not even quite clear to themselves, that what they were building up was not universal truth, but machinery of universal application in the discovery of a certain class of truths. While attributing high and transcendent universality to the central scheme of economic reasoning, I do not assign any universality to economic dogmas. It is not a body of concrete truth, but an engine for the discovery of concrete truth.' (Marshall, quoted in X:196)

But Keynes regretted that Marshall did not actually follow his own precept, and he regarded Marshall's theories as deterministic (X:199). In the above quote, Keynes noted, Marshall was complaining about socialist economics, and he did not apply the moral to his own method.

The Celestial System of Economics

The main point is that Keynes did not believe that the whole economic system could be represented in principle by a set of simultaneous equations. A mathematical system that expressed his economic theory would have to be suited to modelling Chaos as well as allowing the variables to change their meanings in mid-stream. 'The material to which it [economics] is applied is, in too many respects, not homogeneous through time' (XIV:296). I have stressed the point because Keynesian economics was discredited when it was translated into a mathematical system which was found to be defective.

Keynes attributed the general idea of 'a whole Copernican system, by which all of the elements of the economic universe are kept in their places by mutual counterpoise and interaction' (X:205), to Alfred Marshall. 'Just as the motion of every body in the solar system', Marshall had said, 'affects and is affected by the motion of every other, so it is with the elements of the problem of political economy.' But unknown to Keynes, in 1871, one year before Marshall wrote that sentence, Léon Walras had developed an economic theory which actually was inspired by a treatise on celestial mechanics. Unlike Marshall, Walras conceived of a single embracing economic *theory* which could cover the whole economic universe.

A corollary to this unbounded celestial theory is Walras's Law, which says that, if all but one of the markets in the economic universe is known, then the last one, whatever it might be, can be mathematically deduced from the others. This law is in direct contradiction with Keynes's theory, because, whereas Keynes said in the *General Theory* that the rate of interest depends *only* on what happens in the money market, Walras's Law means that a macroeconomic theory cannot be cast in terms of just one market, because everything in the economic universe influences everything else. According to Walras's Law, the money market could be left out of economic theory and the interest rate could be explained by the equations of all of the other market orbits. The question was not whether everything in the economy could influence everything else, which all sides agreed, but whether a scientific economics could embrace all the effects.

J. R. Hicks introduced Walras's Law into macroeconomics as part of a criticism of Keynes. Hicks said, soon after the *General Theory*, that the money market can be regarded as the last equation, which is simply omitted from the mathematical solution of the economic system; and, QED, the interest rate can be accounted for in a theory without a money market (Hicks 1936/1982:92).

The ordinary method of economic theory would be to regard each price as determined by the demand and supply equation for the corresponding commodity or factor, the rate of interest as determined by the demand and supply for loans. If we work in this way, the equation for demand and supply of money is otiose—it follows from the rest; and fortunately, too, it is not wanted, because we have determined the whole price system without it. (Quoted by Keynes in XIV:204)

If Walras's Law is true, then, as Hicks implied, Keynes's money rate of interest is only an empty formalism. The interest rate was really set directly by the demand and supply of loans; but Keynes had left loans out of his theory, making the loans market the one orbit to be deduced from all of the rest. It was logically correct, but artificial, to say that the rate of interest was determined in the money market when it was really the price of loans.

But we could equally well work in another way . . . we could allot to the rate of interest the equation for the demand and supply of money. If we do this, the equation for loans becomes otiose, automatically following from the rest. . . . The latter is the method of Mr Keynes. (Quoted by Keynes in XIV:204)

Hicks assumed that Keynes was formulating a theory in the celestial science of economics, whereas Keynes believed that there cannot be an all-embracing economic science, that science is limited by the wealth of possibly relevant detail. Of course, if it were valid to abstract from the detail, to combine great market systems into even greater market constellations, then a celestial system of economics would be more feasible, and so the issue was what degree of consolidation is admissible in economic theory. Hicks had said that the interest rate is determined in the first instance by the demand and supply for loans, but 'loans' is a great congeries of many different things, and in 'Alternative Theories of the Role of Interest', which was written in defence of his monetary theory of interest, Keynes simply dismissed Hicks, because 'the meaning of . . . "loans" is not defined' (XIV:204). He proceeded to analyse the meaning of 'credit', on the grounds that Hicks and other economists had used a portmanteau word to confuse distinct terms, and thereby advance a classical theory of interest.

Hicks treated the moving constellation of interest rates at the centre of the heavens as a single point, but Keynes saw within it a single star much brighter than the others. Keynes's method was to bring that star into his theory, while keeping open his intuition as to whether other stars might come at times to cast a strong influence. In his theory there was not just the one interest rate but a *spectrum* of rates of return on many assets, of which one was more important than the rest.

There is no reason why their rates of interest should be the same for different commodities—why the wheat-rate of interest should be equal to the copper-rate of interest. For the relation between the 'spot' and 'future' contracts, as quoted in the market, is notoriously different for different commodities. This, we shall find, will lead us to the clue we are seeking. For it may be that it is the *greatest* of the own-rates of interest (as we may call them) which rules the roost . . . and that there are reasons why it is the money-rate of interest which is often the greatest. . . . (*GT*:223)

Abstracting from money returns, there were *own* rates of interest on wheat, houses, copper and other assets, all interrelated in an elastic way by differentials which were changeable and which Keynes did not try to explain, because he was concerned only with the more important variables. The significance of the own rate of interest on money, which equalled the liquidity advantage of holding money, was that liquidity preference did not fall as other assets' own rates fell in attractiveness during a slump. Therefore the money rate of interest set a more or less elastic minimum below which other interest rates could not fall.

It is only in this sense that the money rate of interest in the *General Theory* represents *the* rate. It is the most strategic rate, but not the generic rate of interest. A strategic rate implies that the surface economy is real; it is only the most important interest rate in the circumstances, and it does not try to explain everything. The generic rate of interest implies that the hidden underlying economy is real; it is the general rate relevant for the scientific analysis of regular or long-run economic behaviour. It embraces all the rates of interest because it is supposed to capture their essential meaning.

The Conventional Keynesians

The pre-modern philosophy that underlies the *General Theory* is not easily communicable; Keynes's critics did not understand the point of his *Treatise on Money*, wrote Harrod in his biography, but I have suggested that neither did Harrod fully grasp Keynes's idea of indeterminacy. To become assimilable, the *General Theory* had to undergo a perverse translation of its vision into the methods of natural science.

Keynes, following a suggestion from Harrod, declared the classical theory to be one equation short because it did not take account of income as a variable influence upon savings. The classical economists saw the economy as a plane when in fact it was a cube. If this were Keynes's only objection to the classical theory, then the obvious response would be to put a third line into the cube, and make the classical theory mathematically determinate. Keynes, who had also stressed that the classical theory of interest was a nonsense theory beyond redemption, did not take that step; but Hicks did. It lead to the *IS–LM* system, the Keynesian theoretical structure, the conventional version of Keynes (Hicks 1937).

We must differentiate between Keynes's monetary theory of interest, which has been supplanted and forgotten, and the *IS–LM* or Keynesian theory of interest, which has taken its place. The Keynesian theory of interest is partly Keynes and partly the classical theory of interest. Classical theory had presented interest as being determined in one market—the savings and investment market—and the Keynesian theory of interest combined this classical theory of interest rates with Keynes's own monetary theory of interest. In the *IS–LM* Keynesian theory, the interest rate is in equilibrium if the demand for money equals the supply of money, *and if* savings equals investment. It was not Keynes's theory, because he anticipated and rejected the Keynesian theory by insisting that the interest rate was unrelated to savings and investment:

I am substituting demand and supply analysis for liquidity instead of that for savings. Marshall you say 'thought interest was determined by the schedule of marginal efficiencies and the schedule of the propensity to save'; he forgot that incomes could change. I am saying something totally different from this when I say that interest is determined by the demand and supply for liquidity. (XIII:550)

His argument continued to the effect that, if there were a change in the propensity to save, there would be no reason thereby to expect a change in the demand and supply of liquidity, and so the rate of interest would not change. The equilibrium of savings and investment would be ensured not by a fall in interest, but only by a fall in employment and incomes.

The *General Theory* was not a simultaneous equation theory, because its line of causation ran in only one direction. Given expectations, the money supply determined interest rates; given expectations again, interest rates determined investment; and investment spending then set the total demand for commodities in the economy. The line of causation was therefore as follows:

$$\text{Money} \rightarrow \text{Interest} \rightarrow \text{Investment} \rightarrow \text{Demand}$$

It was, as Keynes thought it should be, a very lean theory, but it had to be intuitively supplemented by a particular feedback loop, which Keynes called 'backwash'. If demand increased in the economy, there would be more need for money to finance transactions, and this money would be siphoned off from the financial and capital markets. The capital markets would then find money more scarce, and the rate of interest would rise, partly offsetting the initial increase in demand. The extra feedback loop would therefore look like this:

Money → Interest → Investment → Demand

Keynes did not try to represent this feedback loop formally, because he believed that in reality backwash would be inconstant and would fluctuate in force. However, he had to debate against Ralph Hawtrey and D. H. Robertson, who both argued (XIV:12 and 231) that there must be a fatal flaw in the monetary theory of interest if the feedback effect could not be formalized. By formalizing the feedback Hicks ended that line of criticism, and the theory that Keynes had said earlier (XIII:550) was 'totally different' to his own he now found unobjectionable. 'I found it [the *IS–LM* theory] very interesting and have nothing really to say by way of criticism' (XIV:79). However, Keynes added that the feedback loop '*need* not raise the rate of interest', even if it was likely to, and shortly after he reaffirmed the monetary rate of interest (XIV:201). Keynes had not abandoned his theory or his method in favour of Hicks.

The *IS–LM* theory did illustrate the backwash effect, but it was taken out of context and its significance greatly overstated. The theory encouraged the neo-classical economists to extend their mathematical systems to absorb Keynes, and, as Hicks said later (1976:140–1), these extensions never got to the point. However, the neo-classical Keynesians were misled not so much by *IS–LM*, as by their tendency to concentrate on the mechanics of any theory, instead of its spirit. By reducing the *General Theory* to simple equations and slogans, they popularized the theory; but when it was disconnected from Keynes the theory was illogical, and vulnerable to a classical counter-attack.[3]

For *IS–LM* was an inconsistent combination, and the theory fell into theoretical disrepute, because a long-run *equilibrium* rate of interest that depends on the money supply does not make sense.[4] If there is such a thing as fullest equilibrium, then the equilibrium interest rate should be independent of the money supply. Start with long-run equilibrium and let the money supply change. Abstract from problems of subnormal dispersion the problem of who gets the extra money—the rich, the poor or the enterprising; assume that all changes are eventually worked out through the economy; assume that there are no other changes in the meantime, and that everyone knows that there are no other changes; then the eventual interest rate will be unaffected by the money supply. Multiplying the money supply a hundredfold should not affect the underlying situation, as Ricardo has said. The only question is whether it is meaningful or profitable to think in such abstract equilibrium terms. The *IS–LM* system was a bastard theory, as Joan Robinson called it, because it drew upon two opposing philosophies to formulate a theory that was consistent with neither of them. The significance of this was that the *IS–LM* theory, with all its contradictions, became official Keynesianism, the rationale to regulate the macroeconomies of the world.

After the Keynesians

When economists realized that the *IS–LM* Keynesian system did not make sense, they first turned to the economics of Hume, which Don Patinkin had refurbished (Patinkin 1965). Patinkin assumed that there is a long-run equilibrium in the economy which is unblurred by uncertainty and independent of money, but he recognized nevertheless that the economy is not usually at this equilibrium, that we have our being in the transition. He believed that Keynes had taken a theoretical snapshot of the transition, without realizing that the economy was on its way to a definite equilibrium according to mathematical laws.

This new version of an old classical theory treated money as just another commodity and assumed that there is a natural rate of interest which must be reached for full economic equilibrium. It was recognized that there would normally be financial movements around the natural interest rate, and unemployment was said to arise from the time the economy took to get to its natural level, but in the long run the real economy was independent of the amount of money. But while Patinkin believed that he had generalized Keynes's *General Theory*, he had really taken a step away from its new spirit; for a theory that assumes away uncertainty is not Keynes's, and Patinkin had reintroduced the underlying real economy, hidden from unscientific eyes.

Axel Leijonhufvud set out to construct a theory based more closely on Keynes, but, again, cast in the language and method of classical economics (Leijonhufvud 1968). As Leijonhufvud put it, the important difference between Keynes and classical economics is that Keynes did not assume 'Walras's auctioneer'; meaning that Keynes did not assume that buyers and sellers know the equilibrium price of anything. He believed that Keynes had understood the economy as a cybernetic system, in which information is not just one more saleable commodity in the system, but is something that influences the *structure* of the system. However, if there is ignorance about equilibrium prices, then prices will not immediately adjust to bring demand and supply together, and quantities in the economy, such as investment and employment, will change as well. Unemployment is therefore due to ignorance and uncertainty.

There is a Keynesian flavour to this theory, and in particular there is a parallel with Keynes's *Treatise on Probability*, with which Leijonhufvud was evidently unacquainted. The quantity adjustments which he says arise out of a cybernetic economic system with partial ignorance are reminiscent of how investment is influenced by the objective chance that arises out of Keynes's veil of probability, philosophic ideas which I say have been transposed to Keynes's economics. It is also consistent with Keynes that Leijonhufvud's emphasis is on method and not on the errors of capitalism—he is critical of attempts to fit Keynes into a deterministic clockwork system, and in his account uncertainty arises out of the nature of knowledge in general, rather than out of the capitalist class struggle.

Nevertheless, Leijonhufvud nowhere acknowledged that Keynes primarily wanted to reformulate economics in terms of a completely different method, and critics have pointed out that he tried to pour his new Keynesian wine into the old classical bottle. 'We have repeatedly referred to the need to discover a basis on which a synthesis of "Keynesian" economics and "Classical" value theory can be achieved', he writes (Leijonhufvud 1968:393), and his theme was that the neo-classical theory should provide the method and Keynes's theories should be the superstructure. 'We have consistently viewed Keynes' contributions to economic theory as part of an overall effort to *extend* the use of the (largely received) tools of general value theory' (p. 333).

Consequently, Leijonhufvud was unwilling to recognize those aspects of Keynes's theories that come most directly from Keynes's own method, such as the influence of speculation and the monetary theory of interest. For example, Leijonhufvud wrote of the monetary theory of interest: 'This notion is a bit disturbing . . . the classical factors of "Productivity" and "Thrift" must still be considered' (p. 174). Later in his book Leijonhufvud denied that Keynes had a monetary theory of interest, and said that Keynes believed in a natural rate of interest, and that Keynes only changed his terminology. 'Although Keynes relinquished the natural rate terminology of the *Treatise*, his position underwent no fundamental change' (p. 349). But the difference between a monetary interest rate and natural rate of interest *is* fundamental, because whether there is a hidden economy underlying the surface hinges on it; and Keynes did not say that he was abandoning the *terminology* of a natural rate, but the *concept* of a natural rate of interest.

I am now no longer of the opinion that the concept of a 'natural' rate of interest, which previously seemed to me a most promising idea, has anything very useful or significant to contribute to our analysis. It is merely the rate of interest which will preserve the *status quo*; and, in general, we have no predominant interest in the *status quo* as such. (*GT*:243)

By putting uncertainty back in the classical bottle, Leijonhufvud puts bounds on the economic system. There is still a river of change, but it only flows between the banks of equilibrium, and these reference points in Leijonhufvud's theory do not exist in Keynes. His attempt to reformulate Keynes led to a theory of Knightian economics rather than Keynesian economics, an economics in which uncertainty is contained.

These neo-classical versions of Keynes, *IS–LM* and the theories of Patinkin and Leijonhufvud, were compromises between logic and common sense, because they did not adequately develop their own assumption that uncertainty and indeterminancy are limited or can be assumed away. If there is no uncertainty, the principle of indifference applies. A new classical economics exploited that assumption to the full with its ideas of a natural rate of unemployment, rational expectations and an optimum quantity of money. For if there will be an economic equilibrium at point X in the future, then we cannot be too far from equilibrium today, being separated only by calculable costs of transition. The effects of subnormal dispersion in the economy can be assumed to cancel out, and the river of change becomes a narrow stream, no wider than the costs of economic information.

If the principle of indifference does not apply, if deviations around an economic mean do not cancel out, if we can make no meaningful quantitative estimate about the likelihood of a war or the price of copper ten years hence, if we cannot overcome uncertainty by any method however onerous and costly, if we simply do not know the future—then Keynes's economics would come into its own again. Yet if the principle of indifference and all that goes with it does apply, it is logical that this principle should be exploited fully. Keynes did not argue that Ricardo was illogical in his own context, but to the contrary, he faintly praised Ricardo, because Ricardo alone could follow his logic so unwaveringly.

Ricardo offers us the supreme intellectual achievement, unattainable by weaker spirits, of adopting a hypothetical world remote from experience as though it were the world of experience and then living in it consistently. With most of his successors common sense cannot help breaking in—with injury to their logical consistency. (*GT*:192)

In the *Treatise on Probability*, Keynes tried to steer a middle course between Hume and Laplace, between reaching no probable conclusion and reaching probable conclusions too superficially. I believe that the misinterpretation of his middle course in probability has led to the loss of his middle ground in macroeconomics. In any event, the shade of Ricardo has returned. It came with the neo-Keynesians, when they treated the process of transition in a capitalist economy as sub-rational. The new classical economics has brought back Ricardo in another form, on the phantasmagoric wings of Laplacian method.[5]

The approach of the conventional Keynesians was useful and pragmatic in the sense that it made macroeconomic management a politically comprehensible and definite task, the adjustment of the economy from one hypothetical equilibrium to another and better one. However, unlike Keynes, they made no allowance for human folly and ignorance in their theories, and they implicated Keynes's system with their own theoretical inconsistency and philosophical shallowness. Despite their apparent success, despite their reputed pragmatism, the Keynesians had no valid defence against the monetarist logic. The conventional Keynesian school was open to the criticism that its full employment policies could only aggravate a natural level of unemployment, while its central economic management, without reference to a vision or a moral concept, was anti-democratic and elitist.

Econometrics*

Econometrics is the statistical measurement of economic quantities, and mathematical economics is economic theory in mathematical form, without necessarily specifying the quantities. I have suggested that Keynes's attack on mathematical economics in the *General Theory* was an indispensible part of the *Theory*. This runs against the received wisdom, because the validity of mathematical economics is not a serious issue among economists, the general view being that whatever can be said in words can also be said in symbols with greater precision and generality. However, economists *do* have reservations about econometrics, which they think is scientific and yet suspect. For example, although Patinkin simply dismisses Keynes's criticisms of mathematical economics, he is supportive of his criticisms of econometrics (Patinkin 1982).

Consequently, while Keynes's objections to mathematical economics have not been seriously analysed, his objections to econometrics have been analysed at length. Yet Keynes had two objections to econometrics which have not been separated out in the literature. Because these two principles have not been identified, his objections to econometrics have been understood only in particular terms, such as to specification bias, or simultaneous equation bias, whereas the matter can be put in a more simple and general way. The theoretically more fundamental objections to econometrics reduce to his objections to mathematical economics; his practical objections to econometrics arise from his objections to Laplacian methods, that is, to the frequency theory of probability which assumes away the limitations of the principle of indifference. Keynes's objections to econometrics reduce to his objections to classical economics.

Keynes opposed false abstraction and the principle of in-difference, but his opposition was not to induction or quantification as such, as his discussion with Harrod of Tinbergen's econometric methods clearly shows. Harrod wrote to Keynes, expressing the

* This section may be omitted on a first reading. Its purpose is to show that Keynes's reservations towards econometrics, which have excited scholarly attention, are an aspect of his general economic method, as I have described it in the previous sections of this chapter.

view that 'Tinbergen may be doing very valuable work, in trying to reduce this part of the theory to quantitative terms', to which Keynes replied:

There is really nothing in your letter with which I disagree at all. Quite the contrary, I think it most important, for example, to investigate statistically the order of magnitude of the multiplier, and to discover the relative importance of the various facts which are theoretically possible. (XIV:299)

Keynes's point here was that economics is properly not a pseudo-natural science, with constant co-efficients and definite independent variables. He objected to Tinbergen's econometrics first because Tinbergen was trying to interpret economics as a natural science in which the rules of mechanical inference without intuition would apply.

My point against Tinbergen is a different one. In chemistry and physics and other natural sciences the object of experiment is to fill in the actual values of the various quantities and factors appearing in an equation or a formula; and the work when done is once and for all. In economics that is not the case, and to convert a model into a quantitative formula is to destroy its usefulness as an instrument of thought. (XIV:299)

The fundamental objections to econometrics can be subsumed under the same categories as the objections to mathematical economics in the previous sections, and merely reinforce my argument that Keynes believed the economic system cannot be given a general mathematical representation.

1. The variables tested by econometrics are not in fact independent:

Must we push our preliminary analysis to the point at which we are confident that the different factors are substantially independent of one another? This is not discussed. Yet I think it is important. For, if we are using factors which are not wholly independent, we lay ourselves open to the extraordinarily difficult and deceptive complications of 'spurious' correlation. (XIV:309)

Likewise, there is no valid distinction between the dependent and independent variables (XIV:310). Nothing acts purely on anything else; everything is in a swirl of causes.

2. The relationships being tested are analogical only because we are not dealing with the real atomic units. Therefore the

background to the variables is not constant but is complex and changing:

There is first of all the central question of methodology—the logic of applying the method of multiple correlation to unanalysed economic material, which we know to be non-homogeneous through time. If we were dealing with the action of numerically measurable, independent forces, adequately analysed so that we were dealing with independent atomic factors and between them completely comprehensive, acting with fluctuating relative strength on material constant and homogeneous through time, we might be able to use the method of multiple correlation with some confidence for disentangling the laws of their action. . . .

In fact we know that every one of these conditions is far from being satisfied by the economic material under investigation. (XIV:285–6)

3. Econometrics cannot bring all of the explanatory variables into the tests because there would be neither meaning nor limit to the process. It is impossible because economics is the field par excellence where objective chance applies.

If it is necessary that *all* the significant factors should be measurable, this is very important. For it withdraws from the operation of the method all those economic problems where political, social and psychological factors, including such things as government policy, the progress of invention and the state of expectation, may be significant. In particular, it is inapplicable to the problem of the business cycle. (XIV:309)

From the modern perspective, there is not much point in measuring equations if it is invalid to have the equations in the first place, and so we do not easily think that econometrics can be helpful when mathematical economics is not. We are however implicitly overlooking the limits of probabilistic analysis and according intuition and the commonly accepted facts of behaviour a lower status than science, which Keynes does not. For example, Keynes thought it was valid to measure the income multiplier, but invalid to go beyond a bare statement of the multiplier relationship.

When this is recognized, Keynes's comments do not support those economists who portray his attitude to econometrics as negative; to the contrary, he attributed a more positive role to induction than do the positivists. He did not agree that the role of statistical investigation is only to refute a theory, because he held that induction can add 'weight' to the probability of theories; and he argued extensively against Hume that the repetition of what *seems* the same experiment can add weight to a theory, since the facts are never quite the same, and a slightly new test is always being undertaken. Keynes did not say, as has been suggested, that an economic theory is never testable. Hume had opposed induction because the mere multiplication of instances proves nothing—if all eggs are alike we learn no more from eating one hundred eggs than from eating one. Keynes replied that all eggs are never alike—'Hume should have tried eggs in the town or the country, in January and in June' (VIII:243). The independent variety in the data meant that probabilistic conclusions can be valid, although of course all induction is still based on some intuition about how alike the eggs really are. The general point concerning induction, to draw rather freely upon the *Treatise on Probability*, is that econometrics and quantifiable modelling are valid if the principle of indifference is valid and the processes of objective chance are frozen. If econometrics is to be applicable, there must be some reason for thinking that the probability of an event being due to an omitted variable is as great as the likelihood of that event not occurring.

Put broadly, the most important condition is that the environment in all relevant respects, other than the fluctuations in those factors of which we take particular account, should be uniform and homogeneous over a period of time. . . . For the main *prima facie* objection to the application of the method of multiple correlation to complex economic problems lies in the apparent lack of any adequate degree of uniformity in the environment. (XIV:316)

This is a prima facie objection, not to Hume, but to the Laplacian assumptions that the *Treatise on Probability* argues are less fundamental (VIII:55). Therefore Keynes proposed a practical modification which would be more likely to yield some uniformity and homogeneity of the background material, to make the principle of indifference more applicable and arrest the distortions of objective chance. He suggested that the periods to be tested should be subdivided in such a way that in each one something like uniform conditions could be assumed. 'If they are, then we have some ground for projecting our results into the future' (XIV:316). He drew this suggestion from Wilhelm Lexis, whom Keynes credits in the *Treatise on probability* with being one of the first statisticians to understand the limits of the principle of indifference (VIII:403 ff.).[6]

The subdivision of econometrics into intuitively uniform periods would make economics more difficult because the number of observations would be smaller in each period, but the point that Keynes is making is of quite another order. The Laplacians were right, Hume notwithstanding, in believing that it was possible to obtain knowledge from induction and observation. Their error was in taking a statistical short-cut and overlooking the necessary role of intuition. Intuition must organize the theory that we formulate, and intuition must also interpret the results of that theory. Tinbergen was following the methods of natural science because he was systematically displacing intuition, and all that it implied, with natural science and all that it implied. The fact that he was doing so by a statistical method that was invalid in itself was of course worse.

Therefore econometrics can be valid in a rough way, but there *was* a basic issue in econometrics concerning which Keynes and Harrod disagreed. Keynes did not agree with Harrod that econometrics would be a good outlet for a lot of workers 'not outstandingly inspired' who wanted to find systematic work to do. The true econometrician, according to Keynes, would have 'vigilant observation'—'passionate perception' into the facts— and would practise a rare art.

The object of a model is to segregate the semi-permanent or relatively constant factors from those which are transitory or fluctuating so as to develop a logical way of thinking about the latter, and of understanding the time sequences to which they give rise in particular cases.

Good economists are scarce because the gift for using 'vigilant observation' to choose good models, although it does not require a highly specialized intellectual technique, appears to be a very rare one. (XIV:297)

Keynes regarded econometrics as an art form and based on the intuition. In the end, Harrod too was excluding the role of intuition from econometrics, and Keynes was asserting it.

Notes to Chapter 8

1. Keynes concluded his biography of Edgeworth by depicting him sitting aloft in a heron's nest, 'so as it were he dwelt always, not too much concerned with the earth' (X:260).

2. Patinkin among others suggests that we should not take Keynes's opposition to mathematical economics at face value, because Keynes attempted to express himself mathematically but failed. 'It may have been Keynes' lack of success with such formal model building in the *Treatise* that led him to a more critical attitude. . . . The *General Theory* reveals an ambivalent attitude toward the role of mathematical analysis in economics' (Patinkin 1982:226).

3. When an economic theory is deterministic, there needs to be a technical explanation of unemployment. The conventional Keynesians were not able to resolve among themselves what this mechanism might be. Hicks said that Keynes had assumed a liquidity trap, or minimum floor for interest rates in the economy. Because the liquidity trap meant that interest rates could not fall sufficiently, investment would be limited, and there would be unemployment.

   I agree with Patinkin and Leijonhufvud that Keynes had not ever assumed a liquidity trap at all, and although he did say in passing that such a thing was a possibility, he immediately dismissed it as unlikely. 'But whilst this limiting case might become practically important in future, I know of no example of it hitherto' (*GT*:207). Hicks needed to invent the liquidity trap to translate Keynes into mathematics; it was his way of reconciling the classical method with some of the flavour of Keynes's monetary theory of interest. If there was a liquidity trap, the rate of interest could still be determined exclusively by monetary conditions, but as a special case.

   However, it became apparent that the liquidity trap theory, which fell a long way short of Keynes's idea of the economy as a flux with a principle of indeterminancy at its centre, could not explain unemployment after all. Franco Modigliani showed that, whether or not there was a liquidity trap, there would still be full employment if wages were able to adjust to make labour demand equal to labour supply. Modigliani followed Hicks's method, but in an effort to make the *IS–LM* theory more logical he showed that a liquidity trap is a superfluous assumption. According to his logic, unemployment was due to rigidities in the labour market, such as trade unions, which stopped wages from falling adequately when labour demand fell. Given the method to be adopted, it *was* a more logical theory, but it was a further step away from Keynes, who, as Patinkin and

Leijonhufvud again show, did not think that high wages were responsible for unemployment. Nevertheless, and despite the clear evidence of scholarship, Keynesian economics came to be known among economists as the economics of the liquidity trap and rigid money wages, and the economics of uncertainty and change were forgotten.

4. Although Keynes referred to 'equilibrium' at a number of points in the *General Theory*, I support the usual view that he did not understand the word in the conventional sense. He sometimes did adopt the usual meaning of the word when discussing classical economics (as in *GT*:80), but evidently only for the purposes of the argument, because in XXIX for example he said, 'In a world of uncertainty . . . a position of final equilibrium, such as one deals with in static economics, does not properly exist'. Where the word 'equilibrium' appears with respect to his own theories, it sometimes means a position where demand is equal to supply but price could nevertheless change. For example, there can be an 'unstable equilibrium' (*GT*:269) when demand equals supply but prices race towards either infinity or zero. More generally, Keynes often meant by 'equilibrium' an intellectual organizing principle, determinateness without implying stability. This is how D. H. Robertson understood Keynes (XIV:98); for examples see *GT*:248, XIV:104.

5. 'Ricardo probably deserves chief credit for launching the [quantity] theory' (Fisher 1911:25).

6. As opposed to the economists, Weatherford interprets Keynes not as a critic of statistical method, but as someone who has attempted to rationalize that method, by defining conditions under which the principle of indifference *would* apply. 'Keynes has *at best* achieved a technical revision which eliminates (at least some) logical contradictions and other absurdities from the implications of the Principle [of indifference]—he has *not* fundamentally altered its theoretical position as the source of all numerical probabilities nor justified its basic assumptions' (Weatherford 1982:83).

PART III

Political Economy

9

The Political Ideals

All kinds of Government which suppose great reformation
in the manner of mankind are plainly imaginary. Of this
nature are Plato's Republic and the Utopia of Sir Thomas
More.

David Hume in 'Idea of a Perfect Commonwealth',
Essays, Moral and Political

Keynes's economics of transition implied that the state should
have a large role in the regulation of economic life. His theories
were therefore embraced by socialists as a route to socialism that
could be justified on purely practical grounds. Likewise Keynes
was rejected by the right; and Keynesian economic theory will
probably remain suspect to the right, so long as it is used to
rationalize increasing intervention by the state in economic life.
But Keynes's political theory has been even more misunderstood
than his economics.

It is true that Keynes did not think that there was necessarily a
conflict between liberty and a strong state, but neither did he
think that a strong state, led by a moral vision to intervene in
economic life, implied socialism. He stepped away from Adam
Smith, not towards Marx but towards Burke. The first principle
of his politics was idealism, and a great deal which seems
puzzling or contradictory only falls into a pattern when this is
recognized. Indeed his political idealism lacks the balance which
appears in his economics, because the rational ideal had to
manifest in politics.

Keynes was neither a liberal nor a socialist, at least in the first
instance, because his politics began from his epistemology. Who
should rule depends on the abstract question of what we can
know. He believed that the state should exercise a practical
wisdom in its affairs, meaning a commitment to truth combined

with familiarity with all the details of a case. Beyond this his political beliefs would depend on circumstances rather than political dogma.

Liberalism was not Keynes's Ideal

By traditional liberalism, Keynes meant individualism, which was liberty against the powers of despots, the compact, and toleration rather than the divine right of the Church.

At the end of the seventeenth century the divine right of monarchs gave place to natural liberty and to the compact, and the divine right of the Church to the principle of toleration. . . . In the hands of Locke and Hume these doctrines founded Individualism. (IX:272)

Kings and Church no longer rule, and liberalism is a changing doctrine. Yet although Keynes is almost always described as a liberal, there is no agreement as to what sort of liberal he was. Keynes had the simple liberalism of Locke, says Cranston (1978:110–12); he was an Edwardian liberal, says Clark (1983: 175). Keynes's liberalism was conservative, says Dillard (1946);[1] he was the founder of a new liberalism at the leftward end of the scale, says Lambert (1963).[2] At least we know that Keynes was a member of the Liberal Party; but this did not imply an intellectual commitment, because Keynes also said that 'political Liberalism must die to be borne again with firmer features and a clearer will' (IX:319), and he expressed dissatisfaction with the Liberal Party platform.

The difficulty of defining Keynes as a liberal is analogous to the problem of what sort of dolphin an ichthyosaurus might be. There is a close resemblance externally, but the lines of his intellectual physiognomy were drawn in an older age of the world. His liberalism is difficult to categorize because his attitude to traditional liberalism was deeply ambiguous, the reverse image of his attitude to the politics of expediency. In the past liberalism had been good in its *consequences* because it 'furnished a satisfactory intellectual foundation . . . to liberty . . . [and] was one of the contributions of the eighteenth century to the air we still breathe' (IX:273). Nevertheless, the new doctrine was wrong in its *logic*, because, being based upon ideas of Locke and

Hume, it 'placed the individual at the centre' and was never able to define a satisfactory relationship between the individual and society. 'It was not long before the claims of society raised themselves anew against the individual' (IX:273). Liberalism could not reconcile the individual and society because it was no more than an arbitrarily claimed set of rights, favouring one side or the other, the social or the personal. By comparison, the doctrine of expediency had been correct in its logic, but in Burke's hands wrong in its assumptions and consequences.

Laissez-faire stands for negative liberty from government; socialism stands for positive liberty from economic oppression. Keynes did not opt for the former rather than the latter idea of liberty, but he accepted neither version of liberty as absolute. Socialism and *laissez-faire* 'equally laid all their stress on freedom, the one negatively to avoid limitations on existing freedom, the other positively to destroy natural or acquired monopolies'. Keynes believed that their conflicting principles could only be resolved by a higher principle applied according to the circumstances. For example, the *General Theory* considered the general circumstances of a conflict between macroeconomic regulation and liberty: individualism was a good principle, but it should be somewhat qualified in the circumstances in the interests of full employment.

Keynes ranked the doctrines of liberalism as only means and not as principles, and therefore as never absolutely good and always subject to qualification or rejection. He acknowledged no unqualified case even for religious and intellectual toleration, for although the case for toleration is close to the case for truth, it falls short of it. There is no reason to tolerate error and evil, except that on practical grounds freedom-loving and liberal men have been mistaken when deciding what error and evil might be. Locke, Keynes said, was intolerant of papists, Rousseau excluded atheists from his social contract, and Burke declared them to be the natural enemies of mankind:

It is only during the last century that the notion has got abroad that toleration is an abstract rule, always and everywhere applicable. Erroneous as the notion probably is, it is not without its compensations; so generally is it true that too great a tendency to seek out the exceptions is equally dangerous to the causes of peace and truth. ('Political Principles of Edmund Burke':74)

Toleration is in no sense a universal doctrine, but it would be a good thing for the world if it were always treated as if it were. ('Toleration')

The case for liberty from the state was still a further step away from the truth, and Burkean principles appear more clearly beneath the liberal façade. Keynes did not disagree when Burke described liberty, 'without virtue and without wisdom', as the greatest of all possible evils, although he put a liberal interpretation upon virtue and wisdom. He responded as follows:

It is the old distinction between liberty and license—the same strong principle acting under two aspects that cannot be distinguished internally, but only by reference to the circumstances in which they appear. It is a question on which there is no need for any man to be inconsistent; we all love liberty and revile license, and these are sentiments which commit us to nothing whatever. ('Burke':7)

Keynes followed the Burkean notion that liberty selects and preserves the products of excellence as guideposts for the cultural continuity of the community. Individual liberty 'prefers above everything, to give unhindered opportunity to the exceptional and aspiring' (IX:311). In the *General Theory* liberty is said 'to preserve the traditions which embody the most secure and successful choice of former generations' (p. 380) and to transmit them into the future. Yet the selection and transmission of the choices of former generations justifies not only liberty but also the active state; the 'same strong principle' appears under the two aspects of liberty and the state, the balance depending on the circumstances in which they appear. Keynes's argument for liberty in the *General Theory* is almost identical to his argument for the organic state in 'My Early Beliefs' written only one year later. 'There are many objects of valuable contemplation and communion beyond those we knew of—those concerned with the order and pattern of life among communities and the emotions which they can inspire' (X:449). In the details of the balance between liberty and the state, Keynes departed from Burke, but the principle of a balance was accepted.

The contrast between Keynes's élitist liberalism and the more usual utilitarian liberalism should be stressed, particularly since the modern liberalism associated with monetarism is a return to the Benthamite tradition. That tradition believes that the individual should be free to pursue his own values, and that government is a hindrance and money a help in the pursuit. Whereas Keynes began from a hierarchy of values, utilitarian liberalism begins from the equality of values; and whereas Keynes wanted more economic equality (see below), the utilitarian liberals opposed measures to redistribute incomes. Keynes was well aware of the differences, as for instance when he quoted Archbishop Whately: 'True liberty "is that every man should be left free to dispose of his own property, his own time, and strength, and skill, in whatever way he may himself think fit, provided he does no wrong to his neighbours".' Whately wrote this in his *Easy Lessons for the Use of Young People*, so Keynes commented as follows: 'The political philosophy, which the seventeenth and eighteenth centuries had forged in order to be able to throw down kings and prelates, had been made milk for babes, and had literally entered the nursery' (IX:280).

Keynes believed that the utilitarian notions of liberty were degenerate now that their original good effect had passed, because the underlying idea had been wrongly expressed, the point of liberty being the expression of excellence rather than a moral equality.

Laissez-faire was not an Ideal

As Keynes became more sceptical and his utopia faded, his moral objections to capitalism receded, and he stressed that capitalism meant liberty. The following comments illustrate a drift:

1925 Modern capitalism is absolutely irreligious, without internal union, without much public spirit, often though not always, a mere congeries of possessors and pursuers. Such a system has to be immensely, not merely moderately, successful to survive. . . . Today it is only moderately successful. (IX:267)

1933 The decadent international but individualist capitalism, in the hands of which we found ourselves after the war, is not a success. It is not intelligent, it is not beautiful, it is not just, it is not virtuous—and it doesn't deliver the goods. In short, we dislike it and we are beginning to despise it. But when we wonder what to put in its place, we are extremely perplexed. (XXI:239)

1939   [There is] a profound connection between personal and political
        liberty and the rights of private property and private enter-
        prise. . . . In all ages private property has been an essential
        element in liberalism—a bulwark against the State and a
        stimulus to comfort and culture. (XXI:500)

Nevertheless, *laissez-faire* was neither a moral absolute nor an
ideal economic system. *Laissez-faire* could not be an ideal in
Keynes's system of thought, and since therefore it was only a
means to a higher moral end, it was subject to qualification. He
wanted to use *laissez-faire* to reach an economic state of plenty
which was not *laissez-faire*. Far from it being the best conceivable
state, he believed that *laissez-faire* had been idealized to reconcile
conflicting strands in the ethical theory of Bentham and Hume,
the doctrine that he opposed and held responsible for 'the moral
decay of civilization'.

Although Bentham and Hume had both rejected Natural Law
metaphysics in favour of rational egoism and utility, they had
interpreted their doctrine differently. Hume meant to destroy the
old ethical metaphysics rather than substitute another in its
place—reason being the slave of the passions, a social philosophy
would be a contradiction in Hume's terms. Bentham, however,
formulated a new ethic for society, the aim of policy being to
pursue the greatest happiness for the greatest number regardless
of the effect on the individual. Therefore, while the consequence
of Hume's philosophy was to buttress property and individualism,
the effect of Bentham's was, to the contrary, to promote equality
and altruism. 'Bentham accepted utilitarian hedonism from the
hands of Hume and his predecessors, but enlarged it into social
utility' (IX:273).

The idealization of *laissez-faire* was a 'miraculous union' which
reconciled equality of opportunity with individualism:

The principle of *laissez-faire* had arrived to harmonize individualism and
socialism, and to make at one Hume's egoism with the greatest good of
the greatest number. The political philosopher could retire in favour of
the businessman—for the latter could attain the philosopher's *summum
bonum* by just pursuing his own private profit. (IX:275)

Laissez-faire had been idealized not by economists but by
political philosophers, and it had 'no scientific basis whatever'.
For, while Keynes conceded that *laissez-faire* in abstract theory is

the most efficient way to allocate resources, the theory assumes
away what Keynes regarded as the dominant features of
economic life. It assumes that the processes of production and
consumption are 'in no way organic'; it assumes away imperfect
foresight; and it assumes away the complexities of the economic
system, including monopoly, adjustment over time, externalities
and joint costs. Regarded as a moral system, it assumes that the
ends of life will be adequately pursued by individuals on the
make. *Laissez-faire* is the economic norm only if our political and
ethical theories have already established a presumption in its
favour, and Keynes had no such presumption:

> many of those who recognize that the simplified hypothesis does not
> accurately correspond to fact conclude nevertheless that it does
> represent what is 'natural' and therefore ideal. They regard the
> simplified hypothesis as health, and the further complications as
> disease. (IX:285)

Keynes did not. Historically, and despite popular prejudice to
the contrary, he said, the idealization of *laissez-faire* had not been
accepted by the best minds among the economists, by neither
Mill nor Marshall, but by 'secondary economic authorities' with
suspect political and moral objectives, such as Mrs Marcel, Miss
Martineau, Bastiat, Archbishop Whateley, the Manchester
School and the Benthamite Utilitarians. Their arguments had
been greatly advanced by the manifest corruption and in-
competence of eighteenth-century government, by the unpalatability of mercantilism and later by the nonsensical turgidity of
Marxism; but merely to be familiar with these arguments is to
reject them.

We have not read these authors; we would consider their arguments
preposterous if they were to fall into our hands. Nevertheless we should
not, I fancy, think as we do, if Hobbes, Locke, Hume, Rousseau, Paley,
Adam Smith, Bentham, and Miss Martineau had not thought and
written as they did. A study of the history of opinion is a necessary
preliminary to the emancipation of the mind. I do not know which
makes a man more conservative—to know nothing but the present, or
nothing but the past. (IX:277)

Capitalism was amoral and materialistic. Its only recognized
object in life was to 'crop the leaves of the branches up to the
greatest possible height', which meant eliminating the shorter-

necked giraffes, the results of the competitive struggle being (wrongly) assumed to be permanent. The real case against capitalism was that its false moral theory put business and religion in separate compartments of the soul; the case for capitalism was that by doing so it harnessed rational egoism and so brought closer the rational moral state in which capitalist values could be discarded. For, unlike the followers of Hume and Bentham, Keynes regarded the purpose of the economic system as *moral*. 'If there is no moral objective in economic progress, then it follows that we must not sacrifice, even for a day, moral to material advantage' (IX:268). As we have seen, however, he believed that there *was* a strong connection between economic progress and morals which required the sacrifice of moral progress to economic progress for the present.

When the accumulation of wealth is no longer of high social importance, there will be great changes in the code of morals. We shall be able to rid ourselves of many of the pseudo-moral principles which have hagridden us for two hundred years, by which we have exalted some of the most distasteful of human qualities into the position of the highest virtues. We shall be able to afford to dare to assess the money-motive at its true value. (IX:329)

In summary, Keynes was not committed to *laissez-faire* as a philosophy but he found it useful as a method. He did not believe that it necessarily gave the best result either in one national economy or in the world, and even when he thought it was economically the best he was prepared to forgo material benefit, at times and to an extent, to advance other goals.

Democracy

Keynes agreed in principle with Burke that there is no *right* to universal suffrage, and that the people only have a right to good, but not necessarily representative, government. The people have an ultimate right to assume power only if the government is not good and just. Having accepted the theory, Keynes subverted its effect, by adding that a good government might also be one which gave its citizens the benefits of political power:

The matter could not be put better [than by Burke] and the only possible reply is the assertion that no good which the government can provide compares in intrinsic excellence with the mere possession of direct political power.

Burke nowhere discusses the possibility . . . of the moral power of self-government. ('Burke':52, 58)

However, these quotes do not capture Keynes's ambivalence to democracy. In 'Burke' Keynes opted only conditionally for democracy; the case for or against democracy was a balance of considerations, a choice between the tyranny of a minority and the transient will of a majority. 'There must be no tyrannical power in the State capable of forcing into operation measures hateful to the people', Keynes said; *but*: 'It is most dangerous that the people should, under normal conditions, be in a position to put into effect their transient will and their uncertain judgement on every question of policy that occurs' ('Burke':53). 'It is to be doubted whether any rational and unprejudiced body of men, who were not, to some extent, under the influence of a fallacious notion concerning natural political rights, would ever have dared the experiment of a suffrage little short of universal' (p. 57); but again, 'The disasters foretold by its opponents have not yet come to pass. Democracy is still on trial, but so far it has not disgraced itself' (p. 58).

Democracy had not disgraced itself in 1906 only because, according to Keynes, it had not had time to disgrace itself, and was still led by the old political élites. Twelve years later Keynes concluded, in the *Economic Consequences of the Peace*, that democracy did indeed disgrace itself when Lloyd George was able to put his return to power above ideals. He appealed to the lower and stronger feelings in the postwar electorate, which wanted revenge against Germany, and he was re-elected on the revenge platform. Keynes's argument was that Lloyd George was irresolute rather than vengeful himself, that Lloyd George did not think the electorate would remain vengeful, but thought that, for the purpose of gaining power, anything could be said now, and that various expedients could be adopted later to mitigate the vengefulness that had been temporarily forced upon him. Lloyd George thought that democracy was politically irresolute, so he did not choose, as Keynes believed the old liberals would have chosen, political extinction rather than political injustice (II:91).

Lloyd George, Keynes said, 'is rooted in nothing; he is void and without content'.

In *A Revision of the Treaty* Keynes reconsidered; it may be *democracy* that is void and without content, that has no serious relation to the truth. Lloyd George, he concluded, could reply to Keynes that he was partly captive to the demands of the mob, that nevertheless he acted for the good where he could, and that the best prospect for a democracy is to be lied to and deceived along the right road. Lloyd George may have brought home the best possible result for a democracy, 'seldom expressing the truth, but often acting under its influence', because in a democracy it may not be possible to opt for 'truth or for sincerity *as a method*' (IX:34). If so, we may conclude from the logic of the argument, Burke was right and democracy should be only a backstop against injustice; there is *no* moral power of self-government. But Keynes considered that Lloyd George's hypothetical reply may have been in error, that the electorate may have been debauched, and that in time it would learn that it had been systematically lied to—the matter was left open.

In his political essays in the mid-1920s, Keynes's politics turned from liberal democracy back to Burkean democracy. The political parties should retain an élitist structure, in which decision-making is confined to the top echelon. Democracy should be retained, but only as a power of last resort and 'until the ambit of men's altruism grows wider'. Keynes had concluded that the democratic state is neither resolute nor just.

Keynes opposed political equality because he opposed the equality of values. *Economic* equality led to the rational moral state, but *political* equality, one of the rights of man opposed by Burke, was based on a false materialistic morality, and was arbitrary in origin and tyrannical in effect. I have run some sentences together from the *End of Laissez-Faire* which show how Keynes identified political equality with the (fallacious) rights of man:

Bentham accepted utilitarian hedonism from the hands of Hume and his predecessors, but enlarged it into social utility. Rousseau took the Social Contract from Locke but enlarged it and drew out of it the General Will. In each case the transition was made by virtue of the new emphasis laid on [political] equality.

Rousseau derived equality from the state of nature, Paley from the will of God, Bentham from a mathematical law of indifference. Equality and altruism had thus entered political philosophy, and from Rousseau and Bentham in conjunction sprang both democracy and utilitarian socialism.

This is the second current [apart from Individualism]—sprung from long-dead controversies, and carried on its way by long-exploded sophistries—which still permeates our atmosphere of thought. (IX:273–4)

The only argument for political equality that Keynes recognized as valid was expediency, understanding that word is both its higher and lower senses, which required only that the people should have the Burkean veto power. The possible moral advantage of the exercise of power, Keynes had concluded, was not an advantage at all.

The Guardians

It has often been said that Keynes's political élitism expressed a bias in favour of his own upper middle class. That may well have been its effect, but it was not his intention, which was to retain the method of Burke while modifying his conservatism by purifying his ideals. It is true that we must take seriously a statement such as this:

How can I adopt a creed which, preferring the mud to the fish, exalts the boorish proletariat above the bourgeois and the intelligentsia who, with whatever faults, are the quality in life and surely carry the seeds of all human advancement? (IX:258)

But this quote was a defensive step in an argument, not towards the rule of the intelligentsia and the bourgeoisie, who were still only fish, but towards the classless rule of inspiration. It should be juxtaposed against statements such as this:

His [Burke's] dream of a representative class can never be fulfilled . . . all experience goes to show that no one class can ever adequately represent either the feelings or the interests of the whole. ('Burke':58)

Keynes did not advocate the rule of a *social* class, but he did advocate the rule of truth and ideas. He objected to materialism of all kinds because it failed to appreciate the epistemological priority of ideas, the primacy of the faculty of the mind. He also objected to religious doctrines such as communism and Christianity because they failed alike to appreciate the fact or significance of the inequality of powers of insight, creativity and reason. All people were potentially capable of entering into the land of reason, but some were much closer to its borders.

A genuine political rule of ideas and values over force and deception would require that people in authority be receptive to the subtler inner qualities which are violated by participation in injustice. They would exercise their offices, if necessary past the point where survival was a reasonable prospect, aware of the need to subordinate the self-aggrandizing tendencies of the ego. The rule of ideas requires that public affairs would spring out of a commitment to a spiritual attitude, whether or not it was recognized as such, as in the Platonic state.

There are two distinct sublimations of materialistic egoism—one in which the ego is merged in the nameless mystic union, another in which it is merged in the pursuit of an ideal life for the whole community of men. . . . It has been the peculiarity of some great religious leaders that they have belonged to both classes at once. (IX:254)

Keynes wanted to bring something like this psychology into the service of the state, and initially, in the *Economic Consequences*, he wrote of a Platonic philosopher-king, who would have combined clear ideas and a wide knowledge with a 'lofty and powerful imagination', and who would have been practical and moral at once.

Even in the *General Theory*, there remain suggestive structural similarities between Keynes's political philosophy and Plato; and in certain respects the political philosophy of Keynes can be regarded as a free-form adaptation of Plato to a commercial Republic. Keynes rejected Plato's authoritarian politics, but he accepted Plato's political ideal. In particular, he implied that the political solution was a guardian class unswayed by the venal passions of humanity.

Though in the ideal commonwealth men may have been taught or inspired or bred to take no interest in the stakes, it may still be wide and prudent statesmanship to allow the game to be played, subject to rules and limitations, so long as the average man, or even a significant section of the community, is in fact strongly addicted to the money-making passion. (*GT*:374)

In Plato's *Republic*, a doctrine of motives is presented as the necessary foundation for the political structure of the state. Plato intended to show that the ideal commonwealth required a class of guardians whose exercise of power was a byproduct of their own spiritual quest. The guardians were free to leave their posts and join the commercial class, but Plato indicates that to do so would be to suppress other motives and sensibilities offering a greater prospect of fulfilment. They were to be defenders of the Greek *polis* in war, but they were also to limit the commercial excesses which would otherwise threaten civil stability. They were prohibited from the love of money or the abuse of power. Indeed, one of the reasons for attributing 'animal spirits' to the guardians is that animal spirits were necessary for political action without apparent reward.

One seeming difference between Keynes and Plato in fact shows a close analogy. In the *Republic*, the guardians were to be prohibited from owning property because 'gold and silver they had within, from God'. Keynes believed that the creative energy of his society had been mostly expressed through commerce and science, but he denounced the *love* of money. At various times he declared it to be semi-criminal and semi-pathological (IX:329), and 'the most destructive vice in modern society'. Elsewhere he also described it as one of the most useful vices; but the point is that the investors who had become rational economic men had forfeited their powers of creation and intuitive insight.

Keynes's historical context was England in process from Adam Smith's élitist commercial republic to mass democratic capitalism. He accepted Alfred Marshall's view that the greater part of the 'higher imagination' of the age had previously been employed in business or science. The creative commercial talents of England had developed the nation's exemplary capital structure and productive skills and techniques. Keynes did not believe that England had developed because of the division of labour, or because the market generated the static conditions for economic efficiency. Nor was the force Max Weber's Protestant ethic, according to which capitalism was developed by anxious ascetics who were alienated from a natural life. According to

Marshall and Keynes, England had progressed because of entrepreneurial excellence, because individualists had by an unconscious moral philosophy reconciled in commerce the public and private good.

However, both in the economy and in the political parties, these values were changing and degenerating under the pressure of growing population and scale. In the economy, the attitudes associated with large-scale production and high finance were no longer consistent with the creative and disciplined mind. The new forces included the growing liquidity of investment, the decline of the family company and the short-run profit pressures associated with large capital conglomerations. Worst of all was the manifestation of mass market psychology. In the eyes of the average opinion which now commanded the financial heights, a longer-run view had come to seem 'eccentric, unconventional and rash'. In his *Economic Consequences*, the change in values was the first cause of the 'extraordinary weakness on the part of the great capitalist class, which . . . seemed a very few years ago our all powerful master' (II:150).

Keynes envisaged a politics of virtue which transcended class interests. His programme was to express in the public sphere those virtues that hitherto had been expressed in commerce and science and art. It was to transfer the qualities of a virtual social guardianship from commerce, where they were dying, and where anyway the power of compound interest was now adequate by itself, to the *control* of commerce, where new opportunities for the expression of the same values could be developed and brought out.

The Labour Movement is represented as an immense and dangerous force of destruction, led by sentimentalists and pseudo-intellectuals, who have 'feelings in the place of ideas'. A constructive revolution cannot possibly be contrived by these folk. The creative intellect of mankind is not to be found in these quarters but amongst the scientists and the great modern business men. Unless we can harness to the job this type of mind and character and temperament, it can never be put through—for it is a task of immense practical complexity and intellectual difficulty. We must recruit our revolutionaries, therefore, from the Right, not from the Left. We must persuade the type of man whom it now amuses to create a great business, that there lie waiting for him yet bigger things which will amuse him more. This is Clissold's 'open conspiracy'. Clissold's direction is to the Left—far, far to the Left; but he seeks to summon from the Right the creative force and the constructive will which is to carry him there. (IX:318–19)

[We need] a reformed and remodelled Liberalism, which above all, shall *not*, if my ideal is realized, be a *class* party. (XIX:441)

This is a politics of creativity, in which the Burkean class structure, which implies injustice, was to be replaced by the class that cannot be a self-interested class, the only class that cannot be purposive. The difficulty is that if this class is not feasible, and in Plato it is only an ideal, then Keynes had not expressed the quintessential opposite to Burke after all. He would, despite his intention, and despite his proposed democratic back-stop, have only changed the character of an unrepresentative ruling class.

This picture must be qualified by Keynes's liberalism. Plato's *Republic* was a poetical analysis of the parallels and relationships between the political element and the human. His image of the ideal state was meant to be the integrated person writ large, but it made no concessions to individualism. Common fears and hopes and desires were its ordinary folk, the aspirations of the human quest were its guardians, and wisdom or the awe of the good corresponded to its philosopher-king. The point is that if Plato's analogy were real then truth and reason, and not vested interests, would always rule.

In practice, most people do not willingly accept the laws of the holy state, and with good reason. Any claim to a special receptivity to a moral or visionary truth can be perverted, and few political virtues are not capable of being imitated and outdone by the worst of vices. Plato assumed the philosopher-king would be willingly obeyed, which is a solution with totalitarian implications. The difference between such totalitarianism and Keynes's liberal version of the Platonic state was that, unlike the totalitarians, he did not want a moral transformation to be *directly* effected through political control. 'The task of transmuting human nature must not be confused with the task of managing it' (*GT*:374). The role of the state was to manage an environment of prosperity and liberty, and (towards the end) of tradition, within which the individual could hopefully transmute himself.

The Letter to Hayek

A famous letter that Keynes wrote to F. von Hayek throws more light on how Keynes's ethics underlay his attitude to liberal capitalism. Hayek had argued in his book *The Road to Serfdom*, which is still a minor classic, that any economic planning was a step on the road to serfdom because of the powers that planning conceded to the planners (Hayek 1944:esp. Ch. 6). Instead of regarding the economy as an instrument to achieve certain ends, Hayek proposed that the government should only maintain a rule of law, a virtual economic constitution, within which people would pursue individual ends. He was less concerned with what the particular laws might be than with the fact of the laws, believing that the discriminatory effects of any law on a particular class or group would cancel out in the very long run. Keynes's response to the *Road to Serfdom* began as follows:

The voyage has given me the chance to read your book properly. In my opinion it is a grand book. We all have the greatest reason to be grateful to you for saying so well what needs so much to be said. You will not expect me to accept quite all the economic dicta in it. But *morally and philosophically I find myself in agreement with virtually the whole of it*; and not only in agreement with it, but in a deeply moved agreement. (J. M. Keynes to Professor F.A. Hayek, 28 June 1944, in XXVII:385) (my emphasis)

Although this letter to Hayek has often been quoted, to my knowledge it has not ever been analysed. It remains a puzzle until Keynes's moral philosophy is recognized, whereupon its meaning falls simply into place. If my interpretation of Keynes is correct, then he was in *moral* and *philosophical* agreement with Hayek because Keynes agreed that the rule of law—an emphasis on process rather than purposiveness—should prevail. However, Keynes also believed, in opposition to Hayek, that the way to disseminate the moral and philosophical state of purposelessness was not via unfettered capitalism: it would be advanced by planning the economy in such a way that more people could be released from the most immediate economic pressures. And so Keynes's letter proceeded:

I should therefore conclude your theme rather differently. I should say that what we want is not no planning, or even less planning; indeed, I should say that we almost certainly want more. But the planning should take place in a community in which as many people as possible, both leaders and followers, wholly share your own moral position. Moderate planning will be safe if those carrying it out are rightly orientated in their own minds and hearts to the moral issue. (XXVII:387)

If the psychology of purposelessness could prevail, there would be no road to serfdom because dictatorial actions would by definition be constrained by the moral priority of means over ends. By trying to bring purposelessness into the *economic* system, which was only a *means* to a mind-state, Hayek had confused a state of mind with what could advance that state of mind, which is to say that Hayek had confused the economic and moral issues:

I accuse you of perhaps confusing a little bit the moral and the material issues. Dangerous acts can be done safely in a community which thinks and feels rightly, which would be the way to hell if they were executed by those who think and feel wrongly. (XXVII:387–8)

Keynes did not deny that in the abstract economic planning would add to the powers of dictators, but he nevertheless wanted more planning, because beyond a point the turbulence of *laissez-faire* would weaken the very moral philosophy that was the greatest barrier to dictatorship. By bringing in the principle of purposelessness at too low a level, Hayek had confused the means with the end and so lacked a principle of balance. Consequently, the danger was that his principle would be implemented in an extreme way, leading to intolerable social and economic results, and to the disrepute of the very principle—the absence of purposiveness—which was the real guarantee of freedom.

What we need, therefore, in my opinion, is not a change in our economic programmes, which would only lead in practice to disillusion with the results of your philosophy; but perhaps even the contrary, namely, an enlargement of them. Your greatest danger ahead is the probable practical failure of the application of your philosophy in the US in a fairly extreme form. No, what we need is the restoration of right moral thinking—a return to proper moral values in our social philosophy. (XXVII:387)

To anticipate the next chapter, Keynes's relationship to socialism was highly ambiguous. He was on the same economic path as the socialists who naturally wanted more planning, but he was on the opposite moral path, because they were antagonistic to the rational ethics that alone gave planning validity. The socialists too lacked a principle of balance because they regarded planning as an end rather than a means:

But the curse is that there is also an important section who could almost be said to want planning not in order to enjoy its fruits but because morally they hold ideas exactly the opposite of yours, and wish to serve not God but the devil. Reading the *New Statesman and Nation* one sometimes feels that those who write there, while they cannot safely oppose moderate planning, are really hoping in their hearts that it will not succeed; and so prejudice more violent action. They fear that if moderate measures are sufficiently successful, this will allow a reaction in what you think the right and they think the wrong moral direction. (XXVII:387)

In sum, Hayek was morally right and practically wrong; whereas the socialists were practically right, but they went too far because they had the wrong morals. But Keynes did not just want a different point of balance to the socialists. A different moral system meant a different economic structure.

Notes to Chapter 9

1. '[Keynes's] work in this sense is essentially conservative and oriented towards a preservation of the status quo' (Dillard 1946/ 1983:230).
2. 'Keynes was an extremely left-wing neo-liberal with beliefs approximating those of socialism' (Lambert 1963/1983:362).

10

Socialism and Equality

The State would have to intervene at many points. Yet the structure of a free economy with its scope for individual initiative must be preserved. Keynes remained essentially an individualist. In the twenty years that followed many others have had the same idea; Keynes deserves study because he related it to the fundamental principles of economics and worked out its detailed applications. His work may still prove to be the foundation of a new kind of free economy, if freedom is indeed preserved.

R. F. Harrod, *The Life of John Maynard Keynes*

The paradox that should be before us now is that one of the most effective equalitarians was apparently opposed to equality. Yet I am unaware of any economist, apart from Joan Robinson, who has in recent years referred to Keynes's equalitarianism, and the incongruence of Keynes's ideas on the subject seems to have been resolved by the disappearance of one of its terms. In the years immediately after the Second World War, when economists were less aware of Keynes's politics, they could take his economic equalitarianism for granted. In 1943, for example, the Marxist economist Michael Kalecki did not dispute that the new (Keynesian) macroeconomics would have radical equalitarian implications, his point being only that these implications were *so* equalitarian that a capitalist economy would not dare to adopt them (see Kalecki 1943). The orthodox economist Dudley Dillard, who later wrote a standard textbook on Keynesian economics, interpreted Keynes as saying that the functionless property-earner was a major obstacle to full employment. 'The ever falling rate of interest, which allows capital accumulation to proceed unimpeded, leads to a fundamental change in the social structure of capitalism, the euthanasia of the rentier capitalist, or functionless investor' (Dillard 1946/1983:222).

This was also how Joan Robinson (1975) interpreted Keynes,[1] and quite reasonably so; but in later years Keynes's equalitarianism was forgotten, perhaps because a better notion of his politics was abroad. Paul Davidson briefly says that Keynes thought economic equality was of lesser importance (Davidson 1982:4). Skidelsky is more cautious, but he warns against taking Keynes at face value, and insists that, appearances perhaps to the contrary, Keynes was not an equalitarian (Skidelsky 1987:75). Harrod wrote enigmatically that Keynes 'had no equalitarian sentiment; he wanted to improve the lot of the poor and that quickly . . . but in order to make their lives happier and better' (Harrod 1951:333).

The evidence from the *Collected Writings* runs in only one direction. Those who deny that Keynes was an equalitarian have the far harder case to prove, and their argument must be to some extent that he did not mean what he said. If we do take Keynes at his word, then he wanted more economic equality, as a step towards his economic Utopia:

> We shall use the new found bounty of nature quite differently from the way in which the rich use it today, and will map out for ourselves a plan of life quite otherwise than theirs. . . . Three hour shifts or a fifteen hour week may put off the problem [of adjusting to leisure] for a great while. (IX:328–9)

The difficulty is that Keynes simultaneously held two principles which he regarded as compatible, but which, according to modern political theory, are inconsistent. He advocated— systematically, and not incidentally—both economic equality and political inequality. The new awareness of Keynes's philosophy of political inequality has eclipsed his arguments for economic equality.

Equality

Recent views notwithstanding, economic equality was a long-standing feature of Keynes's politics, beginning with the revolt from Burke. His commitment to political inequality follows the Burkean doctrine of political expediency, because the case for political equality can only ever be conditional and never absolute. However, economic equality was a counter-stroke against Burke's sanctity of property and in favour of the new economic order.

Because Keynes's equalitarianism arose out of his political philosophy, it was more categorical than a diffuse feeling of sympathy for the poor. He advocated the euthanasia of the functional investor, not because that was his value judgement, but because the hereditary transmission of wealth was an archaic feudal hangover incompatible with a creative society (IX:299). More to the point, Keynes consciously provided the theoretical basis for the equalitarian economic policies that have been adopted in Western countries since the Second World War. He advocated, and showed how to implement, a regime that 'deliberately aims at controlling and directing economic forces in the interests of social justice and social stability' (IX:305).

1. By demolishing the theory of the natural rate of interest, which justifies the rate of profit in terms of the productivity of capital and the rewards to saving, Keynes was able to show that the distribution of income was 'arbitrary and inequitable'. The return on capital is related to interest rates, and Keynes argued that these are determined by expectations and psychological factors. Consequently, the relative shares going to labour and capital could, as he also suggested, be changed by policy, without necessarily affecting economic growth. His theory of interest was the basis for those low interest rate policies, pursued everywhere in the decade after 1945, which deliberately eroded private wealth.

2. Keynes's macroeconomic theory was used as a planning basis for the modern welfare state. Government spending would not be restricted, as before, by the availability of government finance, which was always low at times when it was most needed. After the *General Theory*, spending by the government did not need to balance the Treasury budget, but would balance demand and supply in the whole economy, so providing more scope for the expansion of social welfare. In *How to Pay for the War* Keynes first showed how the new macroeconomics could be used to develop an extended social welfare programme:

In the first version I was mainly concerned with questions of financial technique and did not secure the full gain in social justice for which this technique opened the way. In this revision, therefore, I have endeavoured to snatch from the exigency of war positive social improvements. The complete scheme now proposed, including universal family allowances in cash, the accumulation of working-class wealth under working-class control, a cheap ration of necessities, and a capital levy (or tax) after the war, embodies an advance towards economic equality greater than any we have made in recent times. (IX:368)

D. E. Moggridge notes that 'Keynes' proposals lay at the heart of the policy eventually adopted by the authorities, as did his macroeconomic [policy] method' (Moggridge 1975:182).

3. Keynes exonerated the trade unions as causes of unemployment, with major consequences for macroeconomic and labour policy for decades later.[2] 'It is not very plausible to assert that unemployment in the United States in 1932 was due either to labour obstinately refusing to accept a reduction of money-wages or to its obstinately demanding a real wage beyond what the productivity of the economic machine was capable of furnishing' (*GT*:9).

Keynes's equalitarianism should not be overstated, as it was only a means rather than an end and so was subject to qualification. Truth is far above equality and is by no means the same thing; Keynes accused Marshall of debasing his economics by devoting his attention to bettering the life of the poor, instead of following the flow of his intellectual fancy or the hot economic controversy of the day. 'Marshall was too anxious to do good' (X:200), for the working class in particular. Keynes did see 'social and psychological justification for significant inequalities of incomes and wealth' (*GT*:374), because they were a good stimulus to economic growth and a not too anti-social channel for egoism. He also believed that the health of the middle class, 'out of which most good things have sprung', would determine the health of science and art. Yet a theory for full employment, a new theory of economic distribution, the blueprint of the modern welfare state and the exoneration of the trade unions as major causes of unemployment were all major steps to equality. If they are forgotten or disparaged, it is because we live in a world that Keynes partly created.

The strongest argument against Keynes's economic equalitarianism is that he did not envisage a general movement to Utopia, but rather a series of steps. Successive cohorts of people would pass over the threshold of economic necessity into the land of economic freedom, thereby being liberated to assimilate the new ethics.

It has already begun. The course of affairs will simply be that there will be ever larger and larger classes and groups of people from whom problems of economic necessity have been practically removed. The critical difference will be realized when this condition has become so general that the nature of one's duty to one's neighbour is changed. For it will remain reasonable to be economically purposive for others after it has ceased to be reasonable for oneself. (IX:331)

This is perhaps an extension of the politics of Burke, who advocated the enlargement of the sinecured classes. Keynes hoped economic growth would give everybody a sinecure, because the full Utopia, when purposelessness became possible in a real sense, would arrive only after *everyone* had passed beyond the line of economic need.

And yet he was a political élitist who was particularly sceptical of democracy.

The Politics of Power

According to modern political philosophy, which begins with Machiavelli and Hobbes, whichever political group gets power exploits the situation for itself. However, Keynes's programme combined political inequality with economic equality, because he did not believe in the political superiority of power. He recognized that there was a struggle between capital and labour, but he did not think that anything conclusive or good was to be gained from it. He did not regard the class struggle theory as a specifically socialist theory of politics, but understood it as a *materialist* theory of politics, similar to the theory of power in international relations.

Force would settle nothing—no more in the class war than in the wars of nations or in the wars of religion. An understanding of the historical process, to which Trotsky is so fond of appealing, declares not for, but against, force at this juncture of things. We lack more than usual a coherent scheme of progress, a tangible ideal. (X:67)

Keynes criticized the French Prime Minister Clemenceau, whom he regarded as the author of the Versailles policy to crush

Germany. Clemenceau represented the politics of the Hobbesian *bellum omnium inter omnes*, which, believing that each person finds his liberty through power over others, concludes that power must be the supreme principle of the state. Clemenceau 'had one illusion: France: and one disillusion—mankind, including Frenchmen'; 'The glory of the nation you love is a desirable end—but generally to be obtained at your neighbour's expense'; 'The German understands . . . nothing but intimidation. . . . But it is doubtful how far he thought these characteristics peculiar to Germany' (II:21–2). Power is the principle of the state, but as there is no power to overawe sovereign states they must each, for advantage or out of fear, strive to extend their power. Believing that political ideals are irrelevant and the politics of power is inevitable, Clemenceau pursued a Carthaginian peace at Versailles, meaning a peace that would see Carthage (Germany) finally destroyed. In reply, Keynes said that Clemenceau had anticipated neither the coming economic order nor the organic consequences of injustice; and

[Clemenceau] sees the issue in terms of France and Germany, not of humanity . . . struggling forwards to a new order. . . . It happens, however, that it is not only an ideal question that is at issue. My purpose in this book is to show that the Carthaginian peace is not *practically* right or possible. (II:23)

Likewise, the socialists who concentrated on the politics of power overlooked the 'moral and intellectual problems of the future transformation of society'. They wrongly assumed that a conception of the future already existed, and they failed to appreciate that it would have to convince many people. The general error of the materialists was that they separated their logic and their ideals.

The next step forward must come, not from political agitation or premature experiments, but from thought. We need an effort of the mind to elucidate our own feelings. . . . In the field of action reformers will not be successful until they can steadily pursue a clear and definite object with their intellects and their feelings in tune. (IX:294)

But Keynes rejected the politics which says that power is everything, in favour of a politics which says that power is nothing, that ideals are everything. He did not ever formulate a balance between idealism and materialism. In heaven, where only ideas can rule, Keynes's own ideas may have exerted all the force necessary to show Germany that a higher life than militarism is possible. In heaven too, from where the flux of politics can be seen, cultural continuity and the viability of the state are as irrelevant as Keynes originally believed them to be. In heaven, rich and poor will unite to work towards a high and just conception. But down on earth, I agree with Keynes's critics, and cite Keynes himself, that his emphasis on reason and the rule of ideas was unrealistic and superficial. It is too easy to see through the long reaches of history that kings have ruled over people and that self-interest has ruled over kings. Likewise, any modern society evaluates itself according to its inbuilt criteria, which is for example the purport of the neo-Keynesians when they criticize conventional economics as a rationalization for capitalist values. Keynes's politics was the story of Snow White, but it left out the wicked queen and the magic mirror which tells her she is the fairest in the land. Perhaps it was better than a socialist politics, which is only about the wicked queen, but it was still unrealistic.

In defence of Keynes, it may be said that he fought on two fields: one because he envisaged a Europe united by trade and psychic bonds, and the other because he envisaged a prosperous national economy, united by justice and a moral ideal. In each case the idea he opposed, behind combatative nationalism or the class struggle, was the primacy of power, materialism without a higher conception. Against the ideas of history, nationalism looking to the past, socialism to the future, he had only the method of reason.

His intuition of political goals was right, but Keynes over-estimated the weak political force of reason. He always held to the priority of ideas in the field of knowledge, which is a reasonable position to take, especially given his theories of creativity and intuition; but he extended it to the political sphere, believing wrongly that truth, beauty and love could always overcome material force.

In only one way can we influence those hidden [political] currents—by setting in motion those forces of instruction and imagination which change *opinion*. The assertion of truth, the unveiling of illusion, the dissipation of hate . . . must be the means. (II:188)

It would have been more realistic to say that truth and love lead only to themselves and so are powerless to enforce political justice.

Socialism

As the class struggle has been a fundamental principle of socialism since the time of Marx, it can be said definitively that Keynes was not a socialist. Yet I have already noted that Lambert, whose work is very scholarly, puts Keynes on the left wing of politics, and in this he is not alone. Keynes was anti-doctrinaire, said Austin Robinson, 'but he was never anti-socialist' (Robinson 1947/1983:124). Other scholars have located Keynes on the right wing. 'He thought of himself as a radical,' said Elizabeth Johnson, 'but he took a conservative and even archaic view of society' (Johnson 1974/1983:191).

I suggest that the resolution is that Keynes's political theory was both archaic (in structure), as Johnson says, and left-wing (in intention), as Lambert says, and that Keynes expressed this duality with a particular terminological distinction. Keynes often said that he was on the left and yet he often denounced socialism; and the point of this distinction was that Keynes opposed socialist *materialism*. To be on the left was not to be a materialist, but to be a socialist was.

Keynes opposed socialism, but he was sympathetic to many socialist ideals. Burke's mistake had been to seize on the illogical qualities in materialistic liberalism, without considering that this illogical ideology might nevertheless liberate the men who had lived on the husks of feudalism. By comparison, although Keynes thought materialistic socialism was illogical, he wanted, according to the principles of justice, to (eventually) liberate the men who lived on the husks of capitalism.

Being on the left meant that Keynes shared with the socialists a commitment to greater economic equality; he rejected capitalist values; he was willing to countenance government intervention in the economy; and he believed that the purpose of economic progress is the moral transformation of humanity.

However, Keynes disagreed with socialists concerning both the rate of change and the method. He agreed with Burke that revolutionaries typically do not count the transitional costs of revolution. 'These fellows want a revolution for its own sake', Burke had said, emphasizing the utter frivolity of the old liberals. If possible, Keynes went even further: in an advanced and complex society, a revolution could mean widespread death, and he stressed the need for gradualness of any change. In a complex society, we can never be sure of the full outcome of change, which is often not reversible.

In opposition to the *principles* of socialist materialism, he stood for intuition and creativity instead of the qualitative sameness of all labour; for the mediation of the virtues rather than a notion of the social good; for the superior relevance of the contest of ideas to the class struggle; and for the primacy of the distinction between good and evil, rather than the dialectic of the forces of production. In short, he stood for his philosophy of action instead of socialist ideas, and for the principle not of society, but of the creative mind. These differences meant that Keynes sometimes supported socialist goals and sometimes opposed them. Sometimes too, the differences or agreements were according to circumstance, and sometimes they were according to principle. Matters that were absolutes for socialists were technical questions for Keynes, to be determined according to the circumstances, and constrained only by higher principles.

The fiercest contests [about socialism] and the most deeply felt division of opinion are likely to be waged in the coming years not round technical questions, where the arguments on either side are mainly economic, but round those which, for want of better words, may be called psychological, or perhaps moral. (IX:293)

So Keynes regarded the socialization of industry as a matter for judgement rather than dogmatism. Industry that was still strongly motivated was not to be socialized, but tired industries that had lost their entrepreneurial drive were to be subject to social pressures to act for the public good. They were not to be nationalized or otherwise used to advance a socialist state, but they were to be socialized to advance the rule of moral reason. Keynes's socialization did not imply state control or a co-ordinated economic plan, and although the socialized industries were to be 'semi-autonomous', Keynes meant by semi-autonomy only the Burkean democratic backstop against the abuse of power.

Progress lies in the growth and the recognition of semi-autonomous bodies within the State—bodies whose criterion of action within their own field is solely the public good as they understand it . . . I propose a return, it may be said, toward medieval conceptions of separate autonomies . . .

We must probably prefer semi-autonomous corporations to the organs of the central government. (IX:288–90)

Our task must be to decentralize and devolve wherever we can, and in particular to establish semi-independent corporations and organs of administration, to which duties of government, new and old, will be entrusted. (IX:302)

As the economic problem was solved, the idea was to expand the duty part of industry against the purposive part, provided that the economic cost was not too high. The 'public good' referred to above corresponds to Burke's 'happiness of the people' and is unlike the utilitarian 'social good' of Bentham; it means actions in the public sphere in conformity with ethics.

In particular, Keynes did not advocate the expansion of the state through the use of his macroeconomic policies. A Keynesian macroeconomic policy means that the government should run a deficit and expand its spending when there is a shortfall of demand in the economy. If, however, the government runs a deficit at such times, and if it only balances the budget during periods of boom, then over time the state will expand at the expense of the private economy. A Keynesian macroeconomic strategy may therefore be the easiest and most natural way to socialize the economy, but it was not Keynes's policy.[3]

Because socialists breathe the air of materialism, they misunderstand Keynes and the nature of his difference with them. The objections that the American Marxist economist, Paul Sweezy, had against Keynes are typical—Keynes remained a neo-classical economist; he thought that capitalism was the only possible form of civilized society; he never studied the economy in its historical setting; and he could not see the economy as an interrelated part of an integrated whole (Sweezy 1946/1983: 73). More recently, Michael Bleaney (1985:Ch. 1) made similar points, and added that Keynes's theories do not bear upon Marxism.[4] But all of these criticisms, however understandable, are wrong. Keynes was not a neo-classical economist but the formulator of a new economic method; he wanted capitalism to be eventually replaced by a non-Marxist socialism; he was as much an historical utopian as was Marx; and he analysed the economy as part of an organic whole. Finally, if Keynes's economic method is right, then the Marxian method, which includes the long-run dialectic and is based on Ricardo's scientific approach to economics, is wrong. Keynes's world view was as inclusive as that of Marx, although it began from a different point. Keynes's objections to socialism reduce to his objections to materialism and its arbitrary values. Since *laissez-faire* is also materialistic, and also postulates arbitrary values, Keynes's objections to socialism reduce his objections to the philosophy that *laissez-faire* and socialism share in common. Socialism and *laissez-faire* are only 'different reactions to the same intellectual atmosphere'.

I criticize doctrinaire State Socialism, not because it seeks to engage men's altruistic impulses in the service of society, or because it departs from *laissez-faire*, or because it takes away from man's natural liberty to make a million, or because it has courage for bold experiments. All these things I applaud. I criticize it because it misses the significance of what is actually happening; because it is, in fact, little better than a dusty survival of a plan to meet the problems of fifty years ago, based on a misunderstanding of what someone said a hundred years ago. Nineteenth-century State Socialism sprang from Bentham, free competition, etc., and is in some respects a clearer, in some respects a more muddled, version of just the same philosophy as underlies nineteenth-century individualism. (IX:290)

The 'same intellectual atmosphere' underlying both nineteenth-century socialism and *laissez-faire* was the philosophy of Locke and Hume. Because liberalism had failed to reconcile liberty with the claims of society, it became a divided doctrine, one branch of which began with Rousseau and Bentham's social utility, which was in turn a variation on Hume's individual utility. The school of social utility in turn divided, a sub-branch leading to (materialist) socialism. The appropriate construction to put on Keynes's comment that Marx is 'Bentham *reductio ad absurdum*' is not that Keynes thought Marx was a utilitarian like Bentham, but that Marxism presumes there is a social good rather than a transcendental good, or that Marxism is materialistic. I have drawn an abstract based on *The End of Laissez-Faire*, showing how Keynes understood the kinship of ideas between socialism and *laissez-faire*, and how his objections to socialism begin not with Marx but with Hume and the rights of man (see figure).

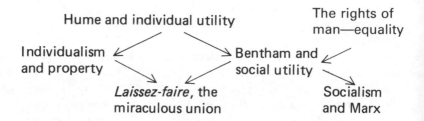

Communism

If, as is usually assumed, Keynes's politics were in material space, and if he really was a participant in the class struggle, then his criticisms of socialism should have signalled an even stronger criticism of communism. To the contrary, shortly after the Russian revolution, Keynes's initial attitude to communism was more favourable than it was to socialism, because he thought that communist values were based on a new morality. Keynes described Russia after the revolution as dull, drab, hypocritical, persecutory and ecumenical, led by men who regarded themselves as exempt from the bonds of truth or mercy. But he was struck by a phrase from Trotsky which referred to the Kingdom of Freedom, and in which, when the revolution had done its work, 'disinterested friendship, love for one's neighbour, sympathy, will be the mighty ringing chords of socialist poetry'. He sympathized with Communist attempts to create a new society with economic plenty but without the profit motive, which was the aim of his own Utopia. The ideals of the West—money and a tired Church—were not true ideals tuned to the new age. The Russians had at least *conceived* of a moral transformation of man through a realm of economic freedom which at the same time was free of capitalist money values.

The moral problem of our age is concerned with the love of money. . . . The decaying religions around us, which have less and less interest for

most people unless it be as an agreeable form of magical ceremonial or
of social observance, have lost their moral significance just because—
unlike some of their earlier versions—they do not touch in the least
degree on these essential matters. A revolution in our ways of thinking
and feeling about money may become the growing purpose of the
contemporary embodiments of the ideal. Perhaps, therefore, Russian
Communism does represent the first confused stirrings of a great [anti-
supernatural] religion. (IX:268–9)

Laissez-faire put business and religion in separate compartments
of the soul, whereas Keynes did not, and Russian communism
did not.

But communism was flawed because it assumed the rights of
man and the equality of values. 'In one respect Communism but
follows the other famous religions. It exalts the common man and
makes him everything. Here there is nothing new' (IX:259).
Keynes took the transcendental road. Unlike the Communists,
he would recognize individualism, so that instead of being
persecutory and intolerant he would harness economic egoism in
the air of truth and freedom. Unlike the Communists, again,
Keynes would base his methods not on the turgid theology of
Marx, but upon a philosophical reason rooted in duty and the
ideals. On both grounds, he opposed communism because of the
inferiority of its conception. Keynes instead would harness the
muscular horse of capitalism to the winged steed of the ideals,
and drive towards a new world. In practice this meant
capitalism, increasingly qualified by equality and a decentralized
moral socialism, and supervised by an active and élitist state.

Notes to Chapter 10

1. Keynes 'welcomed the euthanasia of the rentier. He was only afraid
   that the prospect might be spoiled by failure to get the rate of interest
   to fall fast enough' (Robinson 1975:130).
2. I have quoted this well-known passage from the *General Theory*
   because T. W. Hutchison so strongly denies that Keynes did
   exonerate the trade unions. However, Hutchison's argument does
   not refer to the *General Theory*, and draws only on the 'Keynesian'
   system, which is by no means Keynes's system (see Hutchison
   1981:130 *et seq.*). Whatever the logic of the 'Keynesian' system that
   Franco Modigliani developed, in Ch. 19 of the *General Theory* Keynes

refuted the classical theory of wages, which had provided the theoretical rationale for blaming the trade unions for unemployment. The classical system had not taken account of the effects of changing wage rates upon total demand in the economy.

3. A study of XXVII:264–379 shows that Keynes's recommendation of a budget deficit was in the special context of immediate postwar Britain. He advocated a capital budget to supplement the normal fiscal budget of the Treasury. The capital budget would balance national savings (mainly private) with national investment (which he thought would have to be mainly public). There could also be a deficit in the fiscal budget, but this would be a 'desperate expedient' for the short term.

   It would be stretching a point to depict Keynes's capital budget as a mere rationalization for the government to run an overall budget deficit, although some economists did regard it as such at the time. Keynes's reasoning was that (1) interest rates could not be lowered sufficiently to encourage heavy private investment immediately after the war, but (2) in these very circumstances Britain needed capital formation much more than it needed increased consumption.

   The deficit was to run for about ten years, by which point capital saturation would be adequately reached, whereupon the deficit in the capital budget could be removed.

4. John Eatwell takes a similiar line: 'Keynes failed to present any significant critique of orthodox theory' (Eatwell 1985:37).

11

Conclusion: An Apology for Keynes

> And if there were a contest, and he had to compete in
> measuring the shadows with the prisoners who had never
> moved out of the den, while his sight was still weak, and
> before his eyes had become steady (and the time which
> would be needed to acquire this new habit of sight might be
> very considerable), would he not be ridiculous? Men would
> say of him that up he went and down he came without his
> eyes.
>
> Plato on the philosopher-king, *The Republic*

Keynes's metaphysical vision was that, from the vantage point of
truth and other ideals, economics and politics can be seen as part
of an ever-flowing river of change. Although he applied this
Platonic insight to take account of modern economic progress,
Keynes held, in accordance with his vision, that the correct
beginning in economics is traditional moral and political
philosophy:

Malthus approached the central problems of economic theory by the
best of all routes. He began to be interested as a philosopher and moral
scientist, one who had been brought up in the Cambridge of Paley,
applying the *a priori* method of the political philosopher. (X:107)

Keynes's intellectual paragons, Plato and Burke, the greatest
of rhetoricians, had brought the misty categories of human
existence to bear upon the immediate problems of human
experience. Keynes tried to capture the same range in a way
relevant to the modern world. Like them, he believed that
politics had a basis in ethics, and that, although ideals could not
determine any course of action alone, they necessarily entered
into consideration with the complex facts of particular circumstances. To violate these ideals was at the same time to forgo the

guidance of reason, and to embark upon an unforeseeable flux of political events.

Keynes transposed this principle to economic theory when other economists followed Bentham and Hume and believed in materialism and science. Their philosophy led to classical political economy, the natural science of economics which interprets the economy as a machine. Keynes held that the atomic character of events is complex and uncertain, and that the role of science is to organize material to assist the intuition. Intuition might turn out to be wrong, but in a world dominated by contingency and change there was no reasonable alternative.

Without understanding how literally radical Keynes's theory was, economists tried to express his 'shifting picture of experience' in terms of a science similar to astronomy. This put Keynes's theory into an illogical form, and successive attempts to repair the logic led inexorably to monetarism or socialism, versions of the mechanistic Ricardian economics which Keynes had opposed. The present chaos in macroeconomic theory, with all that this implies for economic policy, has been aggravated by the unwillingness of economists to grasp the elements of Keynes's theory, a fault of the intellectual imagination.

Although Keynes credited Malthus with being the first to conceive economics as an intuitive science, and so the first to understand the need for a general theory of total economic demand, he made two contributions which overshadowed Malthus. First, in his *Treatise on Probability*, Keynes developed the philosophical reasons why economics (which I mention in particular) should not be understood as a natural science. Second, he rigorously applied his own principles and created a formal economic theory, complete with a theory of value, showing how an economic theory might be centred not on equilibrium, but on change itself. Malthus first had the idea, but Keynes gave reasons for the idea and expressed it in an economic theory.

Keynes went further, and by means of his ethical principles linked economic growth to a political ideal, a European civilization ruled liberally in accordance with justice and reason. In practice, this implied the formation of an international economy within which successive social classes would pass from economic need to the spiritually liberating possibilities of art and culture and general purposeless action. His whole political programme, his attitude to capitalism, socialism, democracy and equality, revolved around this utopian and moral prospect. This has been lost by interpreting Keynes as a narrow pragmatist. I have stressed that, for all his insight and intuition, Keynes was, even by his own account, misled by a superficial and exaggerated notion of the power of ideas. Yet this idealism does not implicate his economics. Admittedly, the moral science of economics makes science subordinate to intuition, as does his politics, and gives intuition the same status of reason, as does his politics. Malthus and Burke were the most prominent of the reactionaries and admirers of aristocratic England; and although the intended role of Keynes's vision was to modify their conservatism, while keeping the moral and probabilistic logic of their theory, his political programme would have been strongly élitist in practice.

But Keynes's economics of practical wisdom does not necessarily imply his anti-democratic politics. His economic method follows from his political *philosophy*, which was not inherently anti-democratic. Keynes only arrived at his anti-democratic political *programme* a decade after his political philosophy was formulated, beginning with his disillusionment with democracy during the Great War. Further, although that programme was based on a misconception, it was meant to implement a hierarchy of values rather than of class.

Eventually Keynes recognized that he had not reforged the link between values and policies after all. This was not for the usual reasons. The problem was not that there are no high ideals, or that these ideals must be inconsistent with practical policies. Nor did he believe that ideals must be arbitrary and outside the bounds of political reason. Rather, the political problem began from the 'irrational springs of wickedness' inherent in human nature. This made the ideal economy as well as the ideal political state impossible; but Keynes did not say, as do the moderns, that ethics is meaningless or irrelevant.

The moral science of economics does not mean that Keynesian economics must be arbitrary. It does require reference to values and to the complex facts of a situation; and it does require a process of thought which is not demonstrable as in a logical syllogism. But if uncertainty meant that intuition had to be the criterion, an open liberalism was his method. Keynes does not stand for policy-making by the 'heavy block-head type [who] . . . as they could seldom explain themselves and preferred to rely on their "instincts" could never be refuted' (X:51). He believed that decisions *must* have a subjective element, but not that they must be incommunicable, unarguable or arbitrary.

We still value Keynes's economics if we think that the world is complex and changing; if many elements in a decision, including the likelihood that our own theories are right, cannot be meaningfully quantified; if we suspect that there are events, relevant to most decisions, that are outside our theories and probably outside our frame of perception; and if, given uncertainty, some elements in many actions express a moral quality, because they refer to higher or lower principles. For many of us, these are matters of common experience when decisions have to be made, and yet *only Keynes makes a system of them*. On the surface at least, his economic method is not recondite, but it is no less than the economics of practical wisdom. This too has been lost by interpreting Keynes mechanistically.

Now Keynes's song is fading, and economics is based on materialistic values, or pseudo-science, or ideology and the struggle for power. Once the spirit of his thought began from a high idealism, yet it provided pragmatism with a basis other than the shifting sands of prejudice. It recognized that uncertainty is woven through the fabric of knowledge, and yet it extended the processes of reason to where, it was held, reason could not apply. It gave judgement to matters that were commonly regarded as the preserve of dogmatism, so that Keynes sometimes seemed inconstant and middling, and yet it expressed his commitment to truth, wherever that might lead. His philosophy was *too* sweet and pure, but one of his feet was on the ground and his head was in the sky.

APPENDIX

The Missing Notes on Kant

We have seen that Keynes developed an ethical philosophy which would begin from Hume's identity of probabilistic and ethical reasoning, but would blur Hume's division between ethics and fact. A famous response to Hume's ethics had already been made by Kant; but, whereas Keynes believed that Kant was right to say that a rational theory of ethics was possible, nevertheless, Kant had failed to understand Hume's parallel between probability and ethics. Decades later, Keynes came to believe that there was a particular reason for Kant's failure.

In the course of 1937 Keynes and his former protege, Pietro Sraffa, ascertained that an Abstract of Hume's *Treatise on Human Understanding*, which it had been thought was written by Adam Smith, was in fact written by Hume himself, and that Hume had disguised his authorship. The discovery was not revolutionary, but it clarified some aspects of the *Treatise*, and it was decided to reprint the Abstract with a joint introduction. Soon however Keynes meant to write an introduction that would go well beyond the Abstract, using it as a springboard to criticize Hume for being a congenital liar and for misleading Kant with his lies. This intention was thwarted by Sraffa, who insisted that an introduction to a newly discovered work was not the proper place to accuse the author of being a liar, unless the facts were undoubted, and especially not unless the matter was of great significance, which Sraffa thought was not the case.

There ensued an exchange of correspondence between Keynes and Sraffa and between Keynes and various authorities on Kant, the drift of which is illustrated by the following excerpts.

Keynes to Sraffa, 1 January 1937
Tell me if you think that my footnotes are getting too irrelevant. But I feel this is a production where irrelevance is not altogether out of place.

Keynes to Sraffa, 14 November 1937

I now return to my notes on pages 2 and 2A for which I plead. The story of the disappearance of the *Treatise* during the eighteenth century is of first class interest and importance, scarcely paralleled in the history of philosophy. It comes in I thought, very *apropos* with the disappearance of the Abstract. I do not believe there is any doubt about the facts.

Keynes to the Kantian scholar, Dr E. Rosenbaum, 17 November 1937

I am already having difficulty with Sraffa who is trying to delete everything I have written on Kant on the ground that it is not relevant to put footnotes about Kant in the reprint of a Hume. I am battling with him to preserve at least a number of really interesting details.

Hume had not only disguised his authorship of the Abstract, but had tried for most of his life to suppress the *Treatise*. The *Treatise* failed to attract interest on publication; it was extremely rare even in Hume's lifetime, and no second edition was published until long after. Hume disowned the *Treatise*, which in his eyes was superseded by the publication of his *Inquiry Concerning Human Understanding*. However, the *Inquiry* is now generally regarded as an inferior book, being more readable but less than adequate concerning the logical foundations of Hume's system. On 27 November 1937 Keynes wrote to Sraffa under the heading *Hume's Veracity*:

I have always regarded his [Hume's] statements in regard to the *Treatise* as unreliable. The effect of the violent disappointment he had about that was to ensure a complex in him which prevented him from being sensible on the matter for the rest of his life; his chief object being to cover up and to excuse. On looking into Birbeck Hill I find I am not alone in attributing this side to his character. Hill writes on p. viii of his preface 'Hume, with a levity which is only found in a man who is indifferent to strict truthfulness.'

The letter continues with Keynes detailing various of Hume's lies concerning the publication of the *Treatise*. Here were two philosophers—Hume, who said that there is no rational basis for action, and Keynes, who said that truth is the rational basis for action—and Keynes was accusing Hume of being a liar. What Keynes was driving towards was that not only did Hume lie, but that the spread of his philosophy was advanced by his lies. Keynes's enquiries concerning Kant led him to believe that Kant did not know of the *Treatise* at the time that Kant wrote his famous replies to Hume. Hume suppressed the *Treatise* and favoured the *Inquiry*, and he went so far as to say in the preface to the *Inquiry* that it was the first book that he had ever written.

Keynes to Sraffa, 27 November 1937
As regards Kant . . . my point was that he was not acquainted with the *Treatise* a good many years earlier when he was writing on Hume in the Kritick and the Prolegomena. The point was that Kant was unacquainted with it when he wrote his famous passages on Hume's philosophy.

The point was that Kant had not been able to respond to Hume on Hume's own terms, because Kant had not known properly what Hume's terms were. Kant was familiar with Hume's way of thinking from the *Inquiry*, but he was unaware of Hume's logical structure. Two decades earlier, in the *Treatise on Probability*, Keynes had accused Kant of error, and now it transpired that Hume's deceptions were the reason for Kant's error.

Bibliography

Arendt, H. (1958), *The Human Condition*, University of Chicago Press.

Aristotle, *Ethics*, ed. J. A. K. Thomson, Penguin, Harmondsworth, 1955.

—— *Politics*, ed. T. A. Sinclair, Penguin, Harmondsworth, 1962.

Bleaney, M. (1985), *The Rise and Fall of Keynesian Economics*, Macmillan, London.

Braithwaite, R. B. (1975), 'Keynes as a Philosopher', in M. Keynes (1975).

Canavan, F. (1973), 'Edmund Burke', in L. Strauss and J. Cropsey, *History of Political Philosophy* (2nd edn.), University of Chicago Press.

Carabelli, A. (1985a), 'Keynes on Cause, Chance and Possibility', in Lawson and Pesaran (1985).

—— (1985b), *On Keynes' Method*, doctoral dissertation at the University of Cambridge.

Chick, V. (1985), 'Time and the Wage Unit in the Method of the *General Theory*: History and Equilibrium', in Lawson and Pesaran (1985).

Clarke, P. (1983), 'The Politics of Keynesian Economics 1929–1931', in M. Bently and John Stevenson (eds.), *High and Low Politics in Modern Britain*, Clarendon Press, Oxford.

Cornford, F. M. (1937), *Plato's Cosmology*, Routledge & Kegan Paul, London.

Cranston, M. (1978), 'Keynes' Political Ideas and Their Influence', in A. P. Thirlwall (ed.), *Keynes and Laissez-Faire*, Holmes and Meier, London.

Davidson, P. (1972), *Money and the Real World*, Macmillan, London.

—— (1982), *International Money and the Real World*, Macmillan, London.

Dillard, D. (1946), 'The Pragmatic Basis of Keynes' Political Economy', *Journal of Economic History*, 6; reprinted in Wood (1983, I).

Dobb, M. (1973), *Theories of Value and Distribution*, Cambridge University Press.

Dow, A., and Dow, S. (1985), 'Animal Spirits and Rationality', in Lawson and Pesaran (1985).

Eatwell, J. (1985), 'Keynes, Keynesians and British Economic Policy', in H. L. Wattel (ed.), *The Policy Consequences of John Maynard Keynes*, Macmillan, London.

Fisher, I. (1911), *The Purchasing Power of Money*, Augustus M. Kelley, New York, 1963.

Friedman, M. (1960), 'In Defence of Destabilising Speculation', in R. Pfouts, *Essays in Economics and Econometrics*, University of North Carolina Press, Chapel Hill, NC; republished in M. Friedman, *The Optimum Quantity of Money and Other Essays*, Macmillan, London, 1969.

Harrod, R. F. (1951), *The Life of John Maynard Keynes*, Macmillan, London.

Hayek, F. von. (1944), *The Road to Serfdom*, University of Chicago Press.

Hicks, J. R. (1936), 'The General Theory: A First Impression', *Economic Journal*, 46; reprinted in Hicks (1982).

—— (1937), 'Mr Keynes and the Classics', *Econometrica*, 5; reprinted in Hicks (1982).

—— (1976), 'Some Questions of Time in Economics', in A. M. Tang *et al.* (eds.), *Evolution Welfare and Time in Economics*, Lexington Books, New York.

—— (1982), *Money, Interest and Wages*, Basil Blackwell, Oxford.

Hume, D., *A Treatise of Human Nature*, ed. L. A. Selby-Bigge, Clarendon Press, Oxford, 1888.

—— (1955), 'Of Money', in E. Rotwein (ed.), *David Hume's Writings on Economics*, Thomas Nelson, Edinburgh.

Hutchison, T. W. (1981), *The Politics and Philosophy of Economics*, Basil Blackwell, Oxford.

Johnson, E. (1974), 'John Maynard Keynes: Scientist or Politician?', *Journal of Political Economy*, 82(1); reprinted in Wood (1983, I).

Jowett, B. (1953), *The Dialogues of Plato* (4 vols.), Clarendon Press, Oxford.

Kalecki, M. (1943), 'Political Aspects of Full Employment'; reprinted in M. Kalecki, *Selected Essays on the Dynamics of the Capitalist Economy 1933–70*, Cambridge University Press, 1977.

Kant, I. (1785), *Foundations of the Metaphysics of Morals* (abridged), trans. Louis White Beck, Bobbs-Merrill, Indianapolis, 1959.

Keynes, J. M. (1905–12), The unpublished writings of J. M. Keynes. The Provost and Scholars of King's College, Cambridge, 1988, in the King's College Library.

—— *The Collected Writings of John Maynard Keynes*, ed. D. E. Moggridge (29 vols.), Macmillan, London, 1973–9.

Keynes, J. N. (1904), *The Scope and Method of Political Economy* (3rd edn.), Macmillan, London.

Keynes, M. (1975), *Essays on John Maynard Keynes*, Cambridge University Press.

Kemp Smith, N. (1966), *The Philosophy of David Hume*, Macmillan, London.

Klamer, A. (1984), *The New Classical Macroeconomics: Conversations with the*

New Classical Economists and Their Opinions, Wheatsheaf Books, Brighton.

Klant, J. J. (1985), 'The Slippery Transition', in Lawson and Pesaran (1985).

Knight, F. H. (1921), *Risk, Uncertainty and Profit*, Houghton Mifflin, Boston.

Lambert, P. (1963), 'The Social Philosophy of John Maynard Keynes', in Annals of Public and Cooperative Economy, 34; reprinted in Wood (1983, I).

Lawson, T. (1985), 'Uncertainty and Economic Analysis', *Economic Journal*, 95.

Lawson, T., and Pesaran, M. (1985), *Keynes' Economics: Methodological Issues*, Croom Helm, London.

Leijonhufvud, A. (1968), *On Keynesian Economics and the Economics of Keynes*, Oxford University Press, New York.

Lekachman, R. (1985), 'The Radical Keynes', in H. L. Wattel (ed.), *The Policy Consequences of John Maynard Keynes*, Macmillan, London.

Locke, J. (1690), *An Essay Concerning Human Understanding*, ed. A. S. Pringle-Pattison, Clarendon Press, Oxford, 1924.

Malthus, T. R., *Principles of Political Economy* (2nd edn.), Basil Blackwell, Oxford, 1951.

Marshall, A. (1920), *Principles of Economics* (8th edn.), Macmillan, London; reprinted 1961.

Marx, K. (1954), *Capital*, Vol. I, Foreign Languages Publishing House, Moscow.

—— (1971), *Theories of Surplus Value*, Parts I–III, Progress Publishers, Moscow.

Mill, J. S. (1848), *Principles of Political Economy*, ed. W. Ashley, Kelley, New York, 1969.

Milgate, M. (1982) *Capital and Employment: A Study of Keynes's Economics*, Academic Press, London.

Modigliani, F. (1944), 'Liquidity Preference and the Theory of Interest and Money', *Econometrica*, 12.

Moggridge, D. E. (1975), 'Economic Policy in the Second World War', in M. Keynes (1975).

—— (1976), *Keynes* (2nd edn.) Macmillan, London.

Moore, G. E. (1899), 'The Nature of Judgment', *Mind*, April.

—— (1929), *Principia Ethica*, Cambridge University Press.

Patinkin, D. (1982), *Anticipations of the General Theory*, Basil Blackwell, Oxford.

—— (1965), *Money Interest and Prices* (2nd edn.), Harper International, New York.

Popper, K. R. (1980), *The Open Society and its Enemies*, Vol. 1, *The Spell of*

Plato (5th edn.), Routledge & Kegan Paul, London.

Robinson, A. (1947), 'John Maynard Keynes 1883–1946', *Economic Journal*, 57; reprinted in J. C. Wood (1983, I).

Robinson, J. (1958), *The Accumulation of Capital*, Macmillan, London.

—— (1975), 'What Has Become of the Keynesian Revolution?', in M. Keynes (1975).

—— (1979), *The Generalization of the General Theory and Other Essays*, Macmillan, London.

—— (1980a), *Further Contributions to Modern Economics*, Basil Blackwell, Oxford.

—— (1980b), *After Keynes*, Basil Blackwell, Oxford.

Schumpeter, J. A. (1954), *History of Economic Analysis*, Oxford University Press, New York.

Shackle, G. L. S. (1972), *Epistemics and Economics*, Cambridge University Press.

—— (1974), *Keynesian Kaleidics*, Edinburgh University Press.

Skidelsky, R. (1983), *John Maynard Keynes*, Volume I: *Hopes Betrayed 1883–1920*, Macmillan, London.

—— (1987), 'Keynes' Political Legacy', in A. Kilmanock ed., *The Radical Challenge*, Deutsh Publications, London.

Smith, A. (1759), *The Theory of Moral Sentiments*, ed. D. D. Raphael and A. L. Macfie, Clarendon Press, Oxford, 1976.

Solow, R. (1979), 'Alternative Approaches to Macroeconomic Theory: A Partial View', *Canadian Journal of Economics*, 12.

Sraffa, P. (1951–73), *Works and Correspondence of David Ricardo*, with the collaboration of M. H. Dobb, Cambridge University Press.

Stanlis, P. J. (1958), *Edmund Burke and Natural Law*, University of Michigan Press, Ann Arbor.

Staveley, R. W. (1983), 'Keynes's Adaptation of Classical Economics: An Interpretation', *Australian Journal of Politics and History*, 2.

Sweezy, P. M. (1946), 'John Maynard Keynes', *Science and Society*, 10; reprinted in Wood (1983, I).

Townshend, H. (1937), 'Liquidity Premium and the Theory of Value', *Economic Journal*, 47.

Weatherford, R. (1982), *Philosophical Foundations of Probability Theory*, Routledge & Kegan Paul, London.

Wood, J. C. (1983), *John Maynard Keynes: Critical Assessments* (4 vols.), Croom Helm, London.

Additional Bibliographical Matter

Hession, C. (1984), *John Maynard Keynes: A Personal Biography of the Man*, Macmillan, New York.

Index